PHILOSOPHICAL REFLECTIONS ON THE UNITED STATES CONSTITUTION

A Collection of Bicentennial Essays

Edited by
Christopher B. Gray

PHILOSOPHICAL REFLECTIONS ON THE UNITED STATES CONSTITUTION

A Collection of Bicentennial Essays

Edited by
Christopher B. Gray

Studies in Social and Political Theory
Volume 4

The Edwin Mellen Press
Lewiston/Queenston/Lampeter

Library of Congress Cataloging-in-Publication Data

Philosophical reflections on the United States
Constitution.

(Studies in social and political theory ; v. 4)
Includes bibliographies.
1. United States--Constitutional law. 2. United
States--Constitutional history. I. Gray, Christopher B.
II. Series.
KF4550.A2P48 1989 342.73' 029 88-8862
ISBN 0-88946-104-X 347.30229

This is volume 4 in the continuing series
Studies in Social & Political Theory
Volume 4 ISBN 0-88946-104-X
SSPT Series ISBN 0-88946-100-7

A CIP catalog record for this book
is available from the British Library.

The Edwin Mellen Press
Box 450
Lewiston, NY
USA 14092

The Edwin Mellen Press
Box 67
Queenston, Ontario
CANADA L0S 1L0

The Edwin Mellen Press, Ltd.
Lampeter, Dyfed, Wales,
UNITED KINGDOM SA48 7DY

Printed in the United States of America

TABLE OF CONTENTS

Commentaries:

PREFACE

Christopher B. Gray

Anniversaries are times of nostaglia, and best wishes; centennials more so. But when a bicentennial decade culminates the events wrought in America,[1] whose progeny changed the world--Revolution, Confederation, and at last Constitution--then family feelings must turn into a search for the roots of our successes, and a question why our failures did not reach their potential.

Such radicalism and such teleology have always been philosophers' daily fare. In this book they take their Constitution to its task, and recover those other American philosophers who also set studies to that same task. While taking note of classics from Plato to Hegel, and more on recent American work from Rawls or Arendt or Hauerwas,[2] still they accent American philosophers of the golden age--Peirce and Holmes and Dewey, solving problems in the footsteps of James Madison and Gouverneur Morris.[3]

For that, too, is characteristic of American philosophy. It makes critical inquiries not of neutral issues, but of burning concerns to be remedied. So these authors come forward less as metaphysicians and epistemologists, than as political and legal philosophers, correcting the laws and lampooning the cases;[4] as economic thinkers, seeking the impact of our framers' property interests on the uprightness of our current welfare demands[5]; or as aestheticians and methodologists, opening up new access roads through this academic timber.[6]

For doctrines there are aplenty here, representing our full belief-spectrum--marxian and libertarian, liberal and fundamental, positivist, realist and naturalist. But the discourse of American philosophy is not to utter only the shibboleths of initiates. No, it must always remain accessible, since its high moral purpose is wasted if its words are understood only by the converted. These are inquiries not by the high priests of a philosophical establishment, but mostly from less known teachers and artists, lawyers and journalists. They fit materials useful for professional research and graduate apprenticeship, into a form appropriate also to undergraduate instruction and citizens' reflection.

Not a word of these solutions goes unchallenged. Though we break the silence outside of philosophy, we cannot dominate the discussion once and for all. There is always more to be said, for and against the claims; amplifying and contracting the meanings; disputing the axioms, questioning the process or extending the outcomes. The commentaries in this volume show each of these modes, and form an integral part of the presentations.

Only one study carries the conversation any further, into the reply following its several commentaries.[7] Such an exchange ensued in every other case, too. We desire our readers to continue it, as well. But that one is reproduced here in full, because it formed the plenary session of the conference organized in Philadelphia during the bicentennial year of the U.S. Constitution.[8]

Notes

1. Our celebrations are prolonged, ten years earlier, on this continent with the centennial of the Canadian constitution; and in this hemisphere with the sesquicentennial of the Latin liberations; as well as abroad, a few years later, with the bicentennial of the French Revolution, and the tricentennial of the Glorious Revolution.

2. Clohesy, Sterba, and comments.

3. Botwinick, Fortunoff, Ryder, Waide, Eldridge, Grossman, Kellogg, and comments.

4. Waide, Eldridge, Kellogg, and comments.

5. Ryder, Fortunoff, Clohesy, Sterba, and comments.

6. Botwinick, Grossman, and comments.

7. Sterba, and comments.

8. Thanks to Joseph Betz of Villanova.

THE ARGUMENT OF "FEDERALIST NUMBER TEN"

Aryeh Botwinick

The nature of the problem which Madison proposes to solve in "Federalist Number Ten" is posed in the idiom of ancient and medieval political philosophy. "The instability, injustice, and confusion introduced into the public councils," Madison writes, "have, in truth, been the mortal diseases under which popular governments have everywhere perished, as they continue to be the favorite and fruitful topics from which the adversaries to liberty derive their most specious declamations." Madison thus defines his problem by invoking an anti-progressivist conception of political time. Democratic regimes have been doomed to political instability from time immemorial by the factious predominance of their public councils which causes the political pendulum to swing in a completely opposite direction and leads to the establishment of tyranny as the only means for restoring political order.

As the solution to the problem of staving off indefinitely the destabilizing forces of cyclical political time, Madison resorts to a method which he believes has been overlooked by previous political writers and practitioners. The method consists in the forms of institutional tinkering which enable a designer of states to convert a direct democracy into a republican regime, emphasizing the strategic decision-making role played by political representatives and the prospect of a mutual restraining and cancellation process emerging to blunt the force of factious incursion against the public good which a large society characterized by political representation affords.

There are at least two ways of conceptualizing how Madison believes "republican method" will prove efficacious. The first approach stresses that "right method" consists in fashioning out of the homely materials that go to constitute the nature of one's problem a means to its solution. The solution is only implicitly present in the entities going to compose the nature of one's problem. The precise shape of the solution still has to be teased out of the initial materials by the imaginative investigator or theorist. Republicanism, from this perspective, is a solution that elaborates new possibilities residing in the configuration of the problem. According to a second possible conceptualization, "method" refers to the way(s) a problem is institutionalized so that it can be preserved in its original form as a problem without requiring or provoking solution. From this perspective, the very institutionalization of a problem involves a distancing and containment process which staves off the need for a solution indefinitely. The problem gets played out by being reenacted continually and never needs to be solved in a more overt, official sense. From the current vantage point, to speak of a solution in a context where emphasis is being placed on the search for and application of "right method" is methodologically redundant.

Madison's problem in Federalist Number Ten is twofold: epistemological and practical. Epistemologically speaking, none of the groups tendering claims in the political arena can demonstrate the superior wisdom or justness of their claims in contrast to those of their adversaries and competitors. Madison adopts a Hobbesian and Augustinian view concerning the tainted and limited character of reason: "As long as the reason of man continues fallible, and he is at liberty to exercise it, different opinions will be formed. As long as the connection subsists between his reason and his self-love, his opinions and his passions will have a reciprocal influence on each other; and the former will be objects to which the latter will attach themselves." Madison confronts the dual problem of not being able to rationally adjudicate between the competing claims of different groups and of not being able to contain the power conflicts that result when rational resolution of an absolutist sort has been ruled out. What he proposes to do at this point can be conceptualized simply by saying that he institutionalizes the conflict. He encases it in a more remote setting than that of its original enactment, spearheaded by surrogate advocates--called representatives--in lieu of the original combatants who pressed their claims initially. The transfer of locale and substitution of personnel--the distancing occurring on both levels--allows the conflict to continue without its becoming destructive of either the persons or interests of the original competitors or the institutional structures formed to house and contain their conflicts. From my second perspective, the number and diversity of the advocates is to be seen as a feature of the original conflict-situation itself which is simply transferred to an institutionalized setting and is not an innovation conjured up from the initial materials defining the nature of the problem.

Madison's approach reduces itself to postulating the idea of balance as the appropriate resolution to both his epistemological and power perplexities. "The influence of factious leaders may kindle a flame within their particular States but will be unable to spread a general conflagration through the other States. A religious sect may degenerate into a political faction in a part of the Confederacy; but the variety of sects dispersed over the entire face of it must secure the national councils against any danger from that source. A rage for paper money, for an abolition of debts, for an equal division of property, or for any other improper or wicked project, will be less apt to pervade the whole body of the Union than a particular member of it, in the same proportion as such a malady is more likely to taint a particular county or district than an entire State." What contains religious and political factions is simply their having to confront within a unified institutional setting countervailing factions of an equally insistent sort, which ensures that the residue of deliberation and policy which results from their interaction will more closely approximate to the public interest than any faction's special advocacy taken by itself would. In short, it is the balance struck between opposing forces in an institutionalized setting that serves as the surrogate for Madison for both epistemological certainty and preponderance of power enjoyed by any would-be combatant. In a knowledge and power vacuum, "balance" assigns rewards and distributes penalties. The idea of balance becomes a shorthand way of expressing the primacy of the institutional structure in the achievement of an interim peace.

The idea of method in my second sense as an institutionalization of a problem betrays strong continuity with ancient, medieval and Renaissance conceptions of tacit knowledge. In order to illustrate the nature of the perplexities surrounding the concept of explicit knowledge--and why it is necessary to postulate a dimension of tacit knowledge--it will be helpful to turn to Plato's discussions of these problems in the *Meno*.

> MEN. And how will you inquire, Socrates, into that which you do not know? What will you put forth as the subject of inquiry? And if you find what you want, how will you ever know that this is the thing which you did not know?
>
> SOC. I know, Meno, what you mean; but just see what a tiresome dispute you are introducing. You argue that a man cannot inquire either about that which he knows, or about that which he does not know; for if he knows, he has no need to inquire; and if not, he cannot; for he does not know the very subject about which he is to inquire.

Plato argues that the traditional method for resolving perplexity by proceeding from the problem to solution--engaging in the activities of problem-formulation and problem-solution--rests upon a paradox. One either knows what one is looking for or one does not. If one knows what one is looking for, then the statement of the problem is pointless. If one does not know what he is looking for then a delineation of a problem becomes impossible.

Plato attempts to resolve this paradox by postulating the doctrine that "all inquiry and all learning is but recollection." The very identification and diagnosis of this meta-theoretical problem, however, is suggestive of the scope of tacit knowledge in our intellectual activities. The prefiguration of directions in which to look for solutions to a problem which guides the formulation of the problem in the first place constitute so many tacit pointers which facilitate the articulation of the problem. One might even go so far as to say that Plato's notion of learning as recollection, aside from relating on the literal level to his doctrine of the transmigration of souls, can also be interpreted as a metaphoric expression of the concept of tacit knowing. When one philosophically analyzes what takes place in the activities of intellectual inquiry and learning, these activities appear senseless without the prior postulation of a tacit background which guides and limits inquiry. This tacit background is denominated by Plato--"recollection," but "recollection" one could say simply refers to what has to be presupposed in order to render the current discourse intelligible.

If theories are under-determined by facts, then inter-subjective, hard-nosed criteria for choosing between theories have to be supplemented by less easy to codify, more informal pragmatic criteria relating to elegance, economy and theoretical and practical fecundity. These criteria, precisely because they help determine factual frameworks and are not determined by them, form part of a tacit lore that is transmitted in the course of carefully nurtured apprenticeships served by aspiring students under the tutelage of more experienced teachers. Translated into the personal mode of human relationships, "tacit knowledge" presupposes the participation of new generations of initiates in the practices of judgment of an older generation. It is only through participation that a new generation of practitioners in any particular science or branch of knowledge are able to cultivate the skills in making judgments and exercising connoisseurship which are requisite for the application of tacit knowledge. "The transmission of knowledge from one generation to the other must be predominantly tacit." Since in the end the acceptance of theories and forms of life must be understood as forms of commitment,--and "you cannot formalize the act of commitment, for you cannot express your commitment non-committally,"-- then society must foster participatory environments to enable sane, reasoned commitments to take place, that will ensure the reliable transmission of tacit knowledge and thus safeguard the further accretion of more concrete knowledge.

I have argued elsewhere that Machiavelli and Hobbes continue the tradition of theoretical defense of the doctrine of tacit knowledge and form a more immediate backdrop than Plato for Madison's preoccupation with the concept of "method." The connection between the idea of method in my second sense as an institutionalization of a problem and the concept of tacit knowledge is that "method" represents a solution to a major epistemological dilemma posed by tacit knowledge. By postulating only explicit dimensions to knowledge, one cannot account for how the formulation and transmission of knowledge take place. Problems of interpretation, translation and judgment which arise when knowledge is assumed to be mainly directly formulated in character suggest that on a sheerly explicit level we are bereft of a satisfactory theory concerning how our statements "work." The theory of tacit knowledge calls attention to the way in which any statement that we make appears poised on the brink of being overwhelmed by a boundless range of problems that prevents the statement from getting off the ground at all. The restraining protocols summarized by the notion of tacit knowledge which inhibit an inquirer from thoroughly rationalizing the bases of his knowledge-claims are transmuted by the idea of method in my second sense into a procedure for stabilizing the identity and boundaries of a statement (in Madison's case, the statement of the problem of factions) through externalizing the statement by continual reenactment. Also, Madison's recourse to method renders the statement's philosophical intractability innocuous--the very source of its pragmatically-ordained and achieved solution. It is only because the statement has no philosophical resolution in a narrow substantive sense that it can be resolved in a broader "methodical" sense. The political arrangements of the modern age characterized by the presence of large institutional structures can thus be seen from this perspective as a response to certain key dilemmas concerning skepticism.

The conception of "method" as facilitating the distancing of private interests which enables Madison to make his argument concerning the containment of factions is suggestive of a particular theory of justice and political obligation. The concept of the public is a residual category in Federalist Number Ten. Egotism gets externalized as interest entirely within the confines of the private sphere. Interests are initially articulated and aggregated outside of a governmental setting. Individuals thus evolve their goals and programs in life and determine the means of achieving them in an entirely private capacity. Government is at worst a hindrance and at best a negative regulatory factor in the scheme of the realization of the individual's life-goals. The theory of political obligation implicit in Federalist Number Ten is thus that any state that makes it possible for an individual to realize his interests evokes his allegiance and merits his obligations. Political obligation is directly tied to the furtherance and protection of interests.

The theory of justice evoked by Federalist Number Ten can be labeled procedural justice, in contrast to substantive justice. Considerations of justice come into play to mitigate conflicts between opposing interests and to make sure that no one of them aggrandize itself unduly at the expense of others. Inquiry into questions of justice would proceed on a secondary level, once private interests had been advanced. No preliminary inquiry would be legitimated into the justice of particular claims being present, clamoring for attention in the first place. The theory of justice thus focuses on nonviolation of the rules of the game for the acquisition of property and addresses itself only indirectly to questions of distribution. The subordination of the theory of justice to the theory of political obligation is expressed by the fact that once political obligation is tied to the protection of interest--and a centralized governmental apparatus is requisite to this task--then whatever the state does--no matter what equilibria it strikes between opposing interests--is just. As long as the state is preoccupied with reconciling--or balancing--conflicting interests, it is performing the task for which individual citizens have agreed to obey it.

Given the nominalistic and mechanistic approach of Federalist Number Ten to the concepts of "interest," "the public," justice and political obligation, to impute to Madison the notion that a Marxist elite propertied class is the proper custodian for "the permanent and aggregate interests of the community" would be radically inconsistent. It is the restoration of coherence on the issue of Madison's putative elitism that lends plausibility to Pocock's republican grouping of Madison. Pocock's "tunnel history" of the Atlantic republican tradition renders Madison's concept of "majority faction" intelligible by locating it within the republican system of ideas originating in Renaissance Florence. The dialectic of virtue and corruption--of an ideal projection of social arrangements and its progressive degeneration in the course of getting historically actualized--can get played out by postulating a historically relativized ideal of virtue rooted in the previously dominant intellectual conceptions of the age. The custodian for "the permanent and aggregate interests of the community," therefore, according to Madison, is not a trans-cultural property-holding elite, conforming to the laws of economic determinism but a thoroughly historically rooted Eighteenth

Century elite concerned with perpetuating classical ideals of citizenship and civic virtue. To impute to Madison a Marxist reading of historical development resting upon the unfolding of certain "iron laws" of history violates the skeptical political understandings--the stress on the efficacy of "method" for resolving substantive intellectual problems--voiced throughout Madison's essay. The emergence and functioning of a political elite in a Marxist fashion would also have to be justified in ways that contravene the analysis of interest and the public good incorporated in the bulk of the essay. The virtue of Pocock's interpretation is that it accepts the notion of an elite serving as special custodian of the public interest suggested by Madison's invocation of the "permanent and aggregate interests of the community" at the same time that it accommodates the skeptical political epistemology maintained throughout the remainder of Federalist Number Ten. The political elite's defense of the public interest in terms of its historically relativized republican ideals--historically relativized in the dual sense that they arose in Renaissance Italy and also that they make the process of historical relativization itself central to their understanding of historical development--is entirely compatible with the skeptical understandings of private interest, public interest, political obligation and justice expressed in the essay.

The whole frame of reference in which Madison's argument is conducted has in many ways been superseded by events. A strategy of continual displacement typifies Madison's argument throughout Federalist Number Ten. Passionate egotistic drives are first distanced and objectified into rationally pursued interests and then further distanced and objectified into a multitude of competing interests. The concept of the public interest is displaced from identification with a substantive value or scheme of values onto that shifting set of procedural arrangements that can serve as the optimal accommodation of multiple private interests compatible with the preservation of order. The very conception of the public interest itself has become privatized in Madison's analysis. Madison's concepts of political obligation and justice also presuppose the primacy of a procedural set of arrangements over the state's espousal of particular substantive values.

The background assumption informing Madison's whole argument thus appears to be one of economic abundance. The very resort to "method" to resolve previously insoluble problems concerning political stability presumes the availability and diffusion of resources to enable the continual displacement process to take place. The tab is picked up in the end, as it were, by the prospect of economic reward awaiting those average members of society who have patiently endured Madison's series of displacements.

The transmutation of passion into interest, however, is precarious: it is a historically fragile achievement. The problem of political stability can only get endlessly reenacted instead of permanently solved if there are enough societal resources to facilitate continual entry of new claimants into the political arena as well as the sustained satisfaction of old claimants. Where prospects of economic growth are drastically curtailed, Madison's "methodical" approach will not work. At that juncture, we face the prospects of a regression--of interests getting converted back into passions and the engendering of uncontrollable political instability.

The status quo values of order and stability can be shared by everybody--can form the basis of a nation's political culture--precisely because even the presently disadvantaged members or classes of society enjoy a prospect of economic and social mobility which enables them to perceive stability and order as untainted, broadly supportable values. In accordance with either conceptualization of Madison's problem and his invocation of "right method" discussed in the first part of this paper--whether the proliferation of interests is to be seen as constitutive of the problem or its solution--abundance--or at least continued, incremental growth--is presupposed. Perhaps, one last Madisonian recourse remains available to us in order to salvage his apotheosis of method. Perhaps, the adaptation of "right method" appropriate to our post-industrial age is one which stresses the importance of participation itself--conceived as an egalitarian sharing of power and divorced from the prospect of large-scale economic advance--as the new democratic method--the new institutional reenactment of the problem or the fashioning of a solution out of its homely materials--which promotes allegiance to democratic values when they are severed from possibilities of economic growth and thus buttresses political stability.

MADISON'S "RIGHT METHOD": STRUCTURE OR PROCESS

A Commentary

John Peterman

Professor Botwinick gives us a very suggestive reading of *Federalist Papers*, "Number 10," where Madison presents his argument for rendering factionalism safe for democracy through large-scale representative government. He formulates Madison's problem as how to organize the political state when faced with the skeptical position "of not being able to rationally adjudicate between the competing claims of different groups and of not being able to contain the power conflicts that result when rational resolution of an absolutist sort has been ruled out."[1] Thus the problem is both epistemological and practical. Botwinick claims that Madison responds to both of these concerns by "institutionalizing the conflict," i.e., not eliminating a problem, but creating a process for continually resolving a problem's deleterious effects while continuing to enjoy the beneficial ones. He finds that such institutionalization can only work in a participatory environment grounded in a shared but tacit knowledge, while, reciprocally, such knowledge is also reinforced by the repeated success of the ongoing procedures of the institution's resolution of factional disputes. We will examine further this idea of tacit knowledge taken from Polanyi but will review first Madison's practical solution.

Madison's presentation here is a superb example of political rhetoric in which he offers his planned representative republic as a sedative to calm his audience's fears about the factional strife generally associated with democracies. The newly freed States, although born in violence (and perhaps because of this experience), had as one of their major objectives to avoid the factions which fomented continuing revolutions and instability in the Old World. Europe had been a scene of religious, cultural and class strife for centuries, and Madison well knew his audience's aversion to such turmoil. Hamilton captures this sentiment in his previous *Federalist* essay.

> It is impossible to read the history of the petty republics of Greece and Italy without feeling sensations of horror and disgust at the distractions with which they were continually agitated, and at the rapid succession of revolutions by which they were kept in a state of perpetual vibration between the extremes of tyranny and anarchy.[2]

Madison's problem is how to maintain the healthy pluralism which has provided past democracies with their strength, while at the same time avoiding this factionalism into which this pluralism has repeatedly disintegrated. His strategy in this essay is to make his audience see first that factions cannot be rejected wholesale, as they are a necessary by-product of human liberty, and then that factions can be rendered harmless by creating a process to insure that a majority of extremists (those opposed to the public good or the rights of a minority) can never gain control of the government. His final argument is to show that the representative government proposed in the new Constitution, unlike direct democracies, is able to keep factional disputes in solution and that a large republic does this better than a small one.

Madison suggests that we have two options in response to this factionalism, either to eliminate its causes or to control its effects. To eliminate the causes would be the most efficient approach. These causes include individual liberty and the variety of opinions we entertain, which have other and more important reasons for existing beyond the creation of faction. Liberty is "essential to political life itself," while human fallibility requires that we encourage greater variety among opinions instead of orthodoxy.

Since the causes of faction cannot be removed, "relief is only to be sought in the means of controlling its effects." This relief also could be gained through two approaches.

> Either the existence of the same passion or interest in a majority at the same time must be prevented, or the majority, having such coexistent passion or interest, must be rendered, by their number and local situation, unable to concert and carry into effect schemes of oppression.[3]

As to the first, earlier democratic theorists made the error of believing "that by reducing mankind to a perfect equality in their political rights, they would at the same time be perfectly equalized and assimilated in their possessions, their opinions, and their passions."[4] As Madison finds that this uniformity of possessions, opinions and passions has not yet occurred, he considers it more practical to pursue the second option and offers a scheme of political representation, which based upon a varied and geographically widespread population, would discourage the easy formation of any large factions. A small and homogeneous republic with good communications (like the individual States) could more easily fall prey to the evils of factionalism. "The smaller the society, the fewer probably will be the distinct parties and interests composing it, (and) the more frequently will a majority be found of the same party . . . and the more easily will they concert and execute their plans of oppression."[5]

To counteract this tendency within small republics toward homogeneity and its accompanying possibilities for the tyrannical rule of the majority, Madison feels that "in the extent and proper structure of the Union, as described in the Constitution," which gives authority over aggregate interests to a national assembly and authority over local affairs to the States, "we behold a republican remedy for the diseases most incident to republican government."[6]

In keeping with his skeptical view of humans as "fallible"[7] Madison does not offer us a Cartesian-type epistemological method but rather a practical method, not for reconceptualizing the problem of factions but for rendering them harmless. Although he does propose an "institutionalization of conflict," the actual mechanism for controlling factions seems to be a reliance on poor communications and locally diverse economies to keep interests regionalized. The grand scale of his republic works against the formulation of majorities only so long as it works to keep people apart. The "institutionalization" seems to consist more in limitless expansion, both geographic and economic, than it does in any governmental structure.

Botwinick does seem to recognize this at the end of his essay, but his emphasis on Madison's use of "right method" suggests a focus on structure. As Madison never uses the expression "right method" in this essay, I feel uneasy about this. Madison does use the term "method"[8], but here, as elsewhere, he is appealing to the common sense logic of his audience and not introducing a new way of looking at things. His method, in keeping with his rhetorical purpose, is a very traditional one, exemplified by such expressions as, "In this, as in most other cases, there is a mean, on both sides of which inconveniences will be found to lie."[9]

If Madison's "solution" (or dissolution as Dewey might say) to the problem of factions remains true to his skepticism and his method does remain shy of structure, then does this skepticism also extend to the claim that there are "permanent and aggregate interests of the community" which can be protected and thus must be known? Botwinick turns for help to Polanyi with his notion of tacit knowledge and learning through participation. "When one philosophically analyzes what takes place in the activities of intellectual inquiry and learning, these activities appear senseless without the prior postulation of a tacit background which guides and limits inquiry."[10] This comparison with Polanyi helps clarify an important aspect of Madison's political state. For Polanyi, the openness of knowledge and freedom of inquiry calls for a scientific community with close communication among as many people as possible, while Madison requires a dominance (and thus a separation) of regional interests so that vicious majorities do not arise. All humans can share scientific knowledge in a way that not everyone could share the limited property which Madison set out to protect. The community of knowledge could prove too communal for Madison, as its participants might be inclined to pool society's material resources as well. The "difference of faculties," by which Madison justifies private property as well as explaining the rise of interest groups, could present an argument against his accepting too strong a notion of tacit knowledge.[11]

Polanyi's work, however, does provide an interesting defense for Madison's confidence that future events will be manageable by and consistent with the "permanent and aggregate interests of the community." Polanyi provides the following account of such a self-regulating society.

> Scientific tradition derives its capacity for self-renewal from its belief in the presence of a hidden reality, of which current science is one aspect, while other aspects of it are to be revealed by future discoveries. Any tradition fostering the progress of thought must have this intention; to teach its current ideas as stages leading on to unknown truths which, when discovered, might dissent from the very teachings which engendered them. Such a tradition assures the independence of its followers by transmitting the conviction that thought has intrinsic powers, to be evoked in men's minds by intimation of hidden truths. It respects the individual for being capable of such response: for being able to see a problem not visible to others, and to explore it on his own responsibility. Such are the metaphysical grounds for intellectual life in a free, dynamic society: the principles which safeguard intellectual life in such a society. I call this a society of explorers.[12]

Polanyi's "society of explorers" and Madison's "permanent and aggregate interests of the community" remind me of John Dewey's discussion of the public in his *The Public and its Problems.*[13] Here Dewey wrestles with the same problem which Prof. Botwinick addresses in his concluding remarks, whether great size is still a safeguard for democratic values in an age of great mobility, rapid communications and complex technological problems. Let me conclude with the suggestion that Dewey's public, as a locally-based but also nationally informed community of inquirers pursuing its various interests in a context of shared problems and proposed solutions, would foster the needed "participatory environment" and thus provide a model for the "egalitarian sharing of power" that Botwinick proposes which would be consistent with Madison's credo, "a republican remedy for a republican disease."

NOTES

1. Aryeh Botwinick, "The Argument of Federalist Number Ten." p. 4-5.

2. Alexander Hamilton, John Jay and James Madison, *The Federalist Papers*. (New York: New American Library, 1961), p. 71.

3. *Ibid.*, p. 81.

4. *Ibid.*

5. *Ibid.*, p. 83.

6. *Ibid.*, p. 84.

7. *Ibid.*, p. 78.

8. *Ibid.*

9. *Ibid.*, p. 83.

10. Botwinick, p. 6.

11. "The diversity in the faculties of men, from which the rights of property originate, is not less an insuperable obstacle to the uniformity of interests . . .From the protection of different and unequal faculties of acquiring property, the possession of different degrees and kinds of property immediately results; and from the influence of these on the sentiments and views of the respective proprietors ensues a division of the society into different interests and parties." (Madison, p. 78).

12. Michael Polanyi, *The Tacit Dimension*. (Garden City, NY: Doubleday, 1966), p. 82.

13. John Dewey, *The Public and Its Problems*. (Chicago: Swallow, 1927). Especially Chapter 5, "Search for the Great Community."

PRIVATE PROPERTY AND THE U.S. CONSTITUTION

John Ryder

Documents as historically significant and influential as the Constitution of the United States deserve, perhaps require, ongoing reflections and consideration. Our society would in all likelihood be much better served if public discussion of the Constitution were a more regular feature of social debate and dialogue. In the absence of this, the 200th anniversary of what is arguably one of the most important political documents in all human history presents an ideal opportunity for both a celebration of its achievements and a critical analysis of its shortcomings. It is, I think, vitally important that we not sacrifice appreciation for criticism, nor criticism for appreciation. Failure to take note of the Constitution's accomplishments would make it less likely that we would understand the crucial historical role it played. On the other hand, a failure to subject the document to a careful critical appraisal is to render our present and future slaves to our past, and is to do an injustice to the remarkable social potential still dormant in our society. In the interests, then, of both appreciation and criticism, we will consider some of the political and philosophic problems faced by the Founders, the principles they employed in resolving those problems, and some of the consequences of the product of their labors.

The primary thesis to be developed here, and it is not an original one, is that in confronting the political difficulties of forging a new government, the Founders persistently and consistently employed a class analysis of society in general and of the proper ends of government.[1] While the thesis is not a new one, it is nonetheless a minority view, and the fact that most of the literature which deals with the Constitution and the events and issues related to it has failed to appreciate and employ the Founders' own class analysis has led to serious misunderstandings of the Founders' intentions and of the new form of government they created. The most striking example of this sort of misunderstanding is the view that for the Founders, government is essentially an arena in which a plurality of interests and pursuits interact, and that such interaction should lead, if government is properly constituted, to the greater good of the society as a whole. That this sort of view is indeed a misunderstanding can be seen from the fact, which will be developed below, that the Founders did not regard the many interests of the country's citizens as equally legitimate. Some interests, they thought, were properly to be regarded as rights, while others were necessarily threats to those rights. It was government's task, they held, to protect the former set of interests by preventing the latter from being pursued. What gives the Founders' analyses and the Constitution itself a class character is the fact that the most fundamental issue on the basis of which this distinction between legitimate and illegitimate interests was made was the alleged right to private property. In order to clarify this point and develop its implications, our focus will be on the Founders' own class analysis, the substance of which can be found in the *Federalist Papers*, especially No. 10, and in Madison's *Notes of Debates in the Federal Convention of 1787*.[2]

The Constitutional Convention met in Philadelphia in the spring of 1787 because it was clear to many at the time that the Confederation was not going to be able to meet the very serious challenges which it faced. The threats to the new nation were many and of various kinds. There was the fear, for example, that the English, in alliance with a relatively small portion of the population, would attempt to institute a friendly monarchy in the States, or would at least attempt to manipulate affairs so that the States ultimately formed several small, regional nations, thus weakening what strength even the Confederation had. Furthermore, the nation had for several years been in the midst of a severe economic crisis, and the

Confederation had neither the power nor the resources to respond to the situation effectively. And Shays Rebellion and its suppression at once sent fear throughout the propertied and prominent members of the society, as well as indicating to the more radical faction that a stronger federal government might better be able to protect the interests of society's least prosperous members.[3] In other words, many members of both the Conservative and Radical branches of the revolutionary coalition had their own reasons for wishing to see the Articles of Confederation revised. It is sometimes argued that the Constitution was a betrayal of the principles of the revolution, the genuine defenders of which were the radicals loosely grouped around Jefferson. But it must be remembered that Jefferson and his faction supported both the need for a stronger government and the proposed Constitution itself. The Constitution was not essentially a reactionary document, since its function was to solidify the goals for which the revolution was fought. The support it received from both the revolutionary Right and Left factions is evidence of this.

Despite this general agreement, however, there was still the question as to what sort of society should be created, toward which ends it should aspire, and on which principles the Constitution itself should be based. These were the issues which separated the Jeffersonians and the Federalists, and which made it clear that the various participants in the revolutionary struggle often held widely divergent views concerning the character of the society and government they were creating. Thus, for example, while Jefferson and his faction felt the need for stronger government and generally endorsed the Constitution, they insisted that it be amended with a Bill of Rights. Our concern is to understand what moved the Founders to frame the document in the way they did, and what assumptions they employed in determining the ends they hoped to achieve.

The primary objective of the Founders was to create a government, and a society, which incorporated the maximum degree of individual liberty consistent with the rights of property. They knew, however, that the interests of a large segment of the society, and whatever rights that segment might be thought to have, conflicted with the right to private property. In such a conflict, the people who framed the Constitution argued that property rights must take precedence, and consequently the government they were creating must effectively protect property rights and interests.

Why would the Founders have regarded private property as such a fundamentally important component of society? One answer, which has been popular among some students of the period since Charles Beard's work, is that the people who framed the Constitution were themselves men of property, and they were determined to develop economic, social and political structures through which they could continue to enrich themselves. There no doubt were individuals who saw their task in terms of such narrow financial self interest, but to ascribe such individualized motives to the Founders generally is to ignore, or at least under-emphasize, the historical and theoretical importance of private property in the epoch of bourgeois revolutions and the Enlightenment. Locke, for example, had argued almost a full century earlier and in the context of the triumph of the English Bourgeoisie in the Glorious Revolution, that the unlimited accumulation of private property was a natural right and that the primary object of government was the protection of that right. The Founders, for the most part, agreed with Locke, not merely out of financial self interest, but because they really did believe that there was a *right* to private property, and consequently that any adequate government must protect such a right. The sole dissenting voice at the Philadelphia Convention was James Wilson, from Pennsylvania, who, according to Madison, "could not agree that property was the sole or the primary object of Government and society. The cultivation and improvement of the human mind was the most noble object."[4]

The importance of private property was a central component of the centuries-long struggle by the European merchant class against the power and authority first of the feudal nobility and later the absolute monarch. It was thus perfectly natural for the colonial men of property to take the same view. Further, a right to the unfettered accumulation of the private property is even more understandable in the American context because the Revolution had just been waged in part to rid the colonial economy of the constraints placed on it by the mercantilist policies of the English Parliament and King. The Founders, or at least the Federalist contingent, were economic liberals, and it was not purely by accident that 1776 saw not only the proclamation of the Declaration of Independence but the publication of the *Wealth of Nations* as well. The men who gathered in Philadelphia saw themselves as genuine defenders of fundamental human rights.

Finally, the Founders gave such a central role to property because they believed, as do many contemporary descendants of the classical liberal tradition, that freedom and property both require and imply each other. Madison, for example, in his attempt to show that divergent interests necessarily arise in society says that

> The diversity in the faculties of men, from which the rights of property originate, is not less an insuperable obstacle to a uniformity of interests. The protection of these faculties is the first object of government. From the protection of different and unequal faculties of acquiring property, the possession of different degrees and kinds of property immediately results. . .[5]

Property, Madison argues, is the result of the exercise of differing human capacities, and the freedom to exercise one's abilities is something government must protect. Hamilton, to give one more example of the prevailing view of the relation between freedom and property made the same point on the Convention floor itself: "it was certainly true: that nothing like an equality of property existed: that an inequality would exist as long as liberty existed, and that it would unavoidably result from that very liberty itself."[6]

Given the importance of private property, the Founders faced two major political problems. The first was a result of their view that there is a conflict between the interests of the propertied and those of the unpropertied. The second followed from the fact, which Madison, Hamilton and their colleagues clearly recognized, that since there are different kinds of property, there will necessarily be some divergence of interests among the propertied themselves. We will consider these two issues in turn and in some detail since they are, I think, vitally important for an adequate understanding of the Constitution's handling of the central problem of private property. A failure to appreciate the fact that there are two distinct, though related, issues here has led to considerable confusion concerning the problems which the Founders faced and the political solutions to them which were embedded in the Constitution.

In regard to the relation of the propertied to the unpropertied, the Founders were convinced that the interests of the former were necessarily in conflict with those of the latter. In a passage remarkable for its boldness, Madison makes the point clear: But the most common and durable source of factions has been the various and unequal distribution of property. Those who hold and those who are without property have ever formed distinct interests in society."[7] He made the same point to his colleagues at the convention: "In all civilized countries the people fall into different classes having a real or supposed difference of interests. These will be creditors and debtors, farmers, merchants and manufacturers. There will particularly be the distinction of rich and poor."[8]

The mere existence of conflicting interests would not necessarily present a major political problem. This particular conflict, however, was a fundamental challenge to republican government because the interests of the unpropertied were a threat to property interests which, as we have seen, were taken to involve fundamental rights. The possibility that the majority might use government to pursue its interests was very much on the minds of Convention delegates and men of property throughout the country. On the Convention floor Madison put the point this way:

> In framing a system which we wish to last for ages, we should not lose sight of the changes which ages will produce. An increase of population will of necessity increase the proportion of those who will labor under all the hardships of life, and secretly sigh for a more equal distribution of its blessings. These may in time outnumber those who are placed above the feelings of indigence. According to the equal laws of suffrage, the power will slide into the hands of the former. No agrarian attempts have yet been made in this country, but symptoms, of a leveling spirit, as we have understood, have sufficiently appeared in certain quarters to give notice of the future danger. How is this danger to be guarded against on republican principles?[9]

The same sentiment was expressed by Elbridge Gerry. According to Madison's Notes, "He did not deny the position of Mr. Madison, that the majority will generally violate justice when they have an interest in so doing . . ." That Gerry was speaking here not of any possible majority faction but of the unpropertied majority specifically is indicated in the rest of the passage, where he says that the geographic circumstances of the States make the danger of oppression by the majority less serious than Madison thought it was: "But [Gerry] did not think there was any such temptation in this Country. Our situation was different from that of G. Britain: and the great body of lands yet to be parcelled out and settled would very much prolong the difference."[10]

Gerry was willing to postpone his concern indefinitely, but Madison was not. After pointing out, in "Federalist 10", that a minority faction bent on oppression could be handled without much difficulty, he suggests that a majority faction, interested in the violation of others' rights, is a much more serious matter:

> When a majority is included in a faction, the form of popular government, on the other hand, enables it to sacrifice to this ruling passion or interest both the public good and the right of other citizens. To secure the public good and private rights against the danger of such a faction, and at the same time to preserve the spirit and the form of popular government, is then the great object to which our inquiries are directed.[11]

The interests of an unpropertied majority could be met only by violating the property rights of the minority. Therefore, government must be so constituted as to preserve its general republican form while being an obstacle to the achievement of the interests of the unpropertied.

It was in this context that Madison, Gerry and their colleagues disparaged democracy and attempted instead to develop a form of republican government equal to the task. In one of the early sessions of the Convention, Roger Sherman "opposed the election by the people, insisting that it ought to be by the State Legislatures. The people he said, immediately should have as little to do as may be about the Government. They want information and are constantly liable to be misled." At the same session Gerry said that "The evils we experience flow from the excess of democracy . . . He had he said been too republican heretofore: he was still however republican, but had been taught by experience the danger of the levelling spirit."[12] Madison expresses the same view in "Federalist 10" where he says that democracies "have ever been found incompatible with personal security or the right of property."[13]

The components of the Founders' political solution to this central problem were numerous. In providing for election to certain offices by State

Legislatures rather than by the populace, the Convention was employing what Madison referred to as "the policy of refining the popular appointments by successive filtrations."[14] The property qualifications for the franchise which existed in various forms in different states further served to restrict the electorate to those who were committed to the right of property. But the advantage for the propertied of the new government which Madison emphasized most strongly was its size. It has the advantage, he said, of "the substitution of representatives whose enlightened views and virtuous sentiments render them superior to local prejudices and to schemes of injustice." And he asks "Does it, in fine, consist in the greater obstacle opposed to the concert and accomplishments of the secret wishes of an unjust and interested majority." He answers, of course, that it does: "A rage for paper money, for an abolition of debts, for an equal division of property, or for any other improper or wicked project, will be less apt to pervade the whole body of the Union than a particular member of it."[15] Among the virtues of the Constitution, from the point of view of Madison and many of his colleagues, was that it preserved republican government in a way which would make it as difficult as possible for an unpropertied majority to pursue *its* interests.

The second problem to which property gave rise concerned not the distinction between the propertied and unpropertied, but that between different kinds of property. Madison not only recognized that "those who hold and those who are without property" have opposing interests, but he also saw that within the propertied class itself, different forms of property involve different interests: "A landed interest, a manufacturing interest, a mercantile interest, a moneyed interest, with many lesser interests, grow of necessity in civilized nations, and divide them into different classes, actuated by different sentiments and views."[16] It is quite possible, and probably tempting, Madison thought, for those whose interests lay with one form of property to use the power of government to interfere unjustly with the equally legitimate interests of other forms of property. In "Federalist 10" he offers several examples of what he means:

> Shall domestic manufacturers be encouraged, and in what degree, by restrictions on foreign manufacturers? are questions which would be differently decided by the landed

> and the manufacturing classes, and probably by neither with a sole regard to justice and the public good. The apportionment of taxes on the various descriptions of property is an act which seems to require the most exact impartiality; yet there is, perhaps, no legislative act in which greater opportunity and temptation are given to a predominant party to trample on the rules of justice. Every shilling with which they overburden the inferior number is a shilling saved to their own pockets.[17]

Such activities as these are of course inappropriate and unjust in that they are an abuse of political power to interfere with the legitimate right to exercise one's property. Government, then, must prevent divergent property interests from unjustly oppressing each other. It was in response to this sort of problem that the Founders endorsed one or another version of the separation of governmental powers and the checks of each on the others. In *this* respect it is possible to say that the government formed by the Constitution is an umpire, seeing to it that no one set of legitimate interests and rights over-extends its bounds and unjustly oppresses another set of equally legitimate interests and rights.

It is important that the difference between the two kinds of conflicts be made clear. In the case of the clash between the interests of the propertied and those of the unpropertied, the relevant threat is from an unjust interest, i.e., that of the unpropertied, against a genuine right. In the clash between different forms of property, however, all the participants have equally defensible rights and interests. Thus it is understandable that the Founders would wish to devise a way, in the latter case, for no interest to dominate the others. But such a solution would make no sense in the former case. It would have been impossible for most of the Founders to say that legitimate rights to property should not dominate the unjust interests of the unpropertied. From the perspective of the Founders, rights to property must be protected at the expense of the interests of the unpropertied. Any alternative would be equivalent to abandoning property rights, something the Founders were not inclined to do. Thus the separation of powers and the checks and balances built into the new government were never intended to balance propertied with unpropertied interests. It was taken for granted that the former should prevail. They were, however, intended to balance the interests of the various forms of property. In *that* conflict, unlike the other, all the players were equally entitled to participate and compete. Without an appreciation of this distinction, it is easy to misread Madison and the Founders generally as favoring a political pluralism in which all competing interests have a place. But given their views on property rights and the necessary conflict between propertied and unpropertied interests, such a view is untenable.

The proper conclusion to be drawn from this analysis is, as I suggested at the beginning, both appreciative and critical. Despite the blatant and very serious shortcomings of the government created by the Constitution, such as its tolerance of slavery and its disenfranchisement of women, free Blacks and Native Americans, the documents succeeded in consolidating many of the gains won by the Revolution. The new government effectively eradicated any possibility of a hereditary nobility, and ended whatever hopes some had entertained of establishing a monarchy by mandating that all States must themselves have a republican government regardless of how many citizens may have wished otherwise. The Constitution established as a legal principle even greater religious tolerance and freedom than was the case in several States at that time. And further, it represented in legal form the consolidation of the principles of economic liberalism which allowed in turn the release of the extraordinary power of private capital. All of this, in 1787, was to be admired.

In 1987, however, the principles which informed the Constitution at its inception and which in many crucial respects continue to inform it, are an obstacle to social progress and human development. The point I wish to make was expressed in one way by Jefferson in a letter to Madison dated October 28, 1785. Jefferson was in France at the time, and had been reflecting on "that unequal division of property which occasions the numberless instances of wretchedness which I had observed in this country . . ." He concluded that "Whenever there is in any country, uncultivated lands and unemployed poor, it is clear that the laws of property have been so far extended as to violate natural right."[18]

Madison was quite right, it seems to me, in his view that property rights conflict with the interests of those who own and control no property, no capital. In its essential features the situation has changed very little during the past two hundred years. Private capital today still has the power to control the majority's lives. When it is in capital's interest to close a plant, put hundreds or even thousands of people out of work, and create economic disaster for whole communities, it does so, and it does it with the legal sanction of the Constitution's enshrinement of property rights. When it wishes to extend its domain beyond our borders, and use our public power to assist it in extracting even greater wealth from other people, it does so, again with the Constitution's sanction. When it wishes to break labor organizations to force its own vision of appropriate pay, working conditions, etc., it does so, and the Constitution again permits this in the name of property rights. This sort of litany could go on interminably, and in every case the interests of capital conflict with those of the majority. With respect to that "most common and durable source of factions," the Constitution is today an impediment to progress and to the ongoing attempt on the part of working people to share a more equitable distribution of the fruits of our labor.

NOTES

1. Two of the more noteworthy statements of this perspective are in Herbert Aptheker, *Early Years of the Republic*. (New York: International Publishers, 1976), and Michael Parenti, "The Constitution as an Elitist Document," in Robert A. Goldwin and William A. Schambra, eds., *How Democratic is the Constitution?* (Washington, DC: American Enterprise Institute for Public Policy Research, 1980), pp. 39-58.

2. Roy P. Fairfield, ed. *The Federalist Papers* (Garden City, NY: Doubleday and Co., Inc., 1961). James Madison, *Notes of Debates in the Federal Convention of 1787* (Athens, OH: Ohio University Press, 1976). It should be pointed out here that while the issue of property is a central one in these satellite documents, it is nearly completely absent from the Constitution itself. In fact, the original document endorsed by the Convention in September 1787 makes no mention of private property at all, and the first appearance of the term is in the Fifth Amendment, which says, among other things, that no person shall "be deprived of life, liberty, or property, without due process of law; nor shall private property be taken for public use, without just compensation." At first glance it seems rather odd that a concern so fundamental to the Founders would not be discussed in the Constitution they wrote. But it turns out not to be odd at all. The Constitution is in many ways a "minimalist" document, and its nearly exclusive concern is with the structure and procedure of government. This is precisely the characteristic which makes it appear to be "neutral" with respect to specific social interests. That it is *not* neutral, or at least was not intended to be, is made clear in the various arguments which Madison, Hamilton and others offered in its support.

3. See Aptheker, *op. cit.*, Ch. 2.

4. *Notes*, p. 287.

5. "Federalist 10," pp. 17-18.

6. *Notes*, p. 196.

7. "Federalist 10," p. 18.

8. *Notes*, p. 194. Notice that in these passages Madison refers to the various interests related to property as "distinct" and as a "difference of interests." To say that two things are "distinct" or "different" is not necessarily to say that they conflict or are incompatible. In the case of property interest, however, Madison does think that there is a conflict and an incompatibility. The evidence for this reading of Madison derives from the specific points he makes about these differences, and the several reasons he gives for why these differences present such a serious political problem.

9. *Ibid.*, p. 194.

10. *Ibid*., p. 197.

11. "Federalist 10," pp. 19-20.

12. *Notes*, p. 39.

13. "Federalist 10," p. 20.

14. *Notes*, p. 40.

15. "Federalist 10," p. 23.

16. *Ibid*., p. 18

17. *Ibid*., p. 19.

18. Merrill D. Peterson, ed. *The Portable Thomas Jefferson*. (New York: Penguin Books, 1983), pp. 396-397.

MADISONIAN DEMOCRACY AND MARXIST ANALYSIS: RYDER ON THE CONSTITUTION

A Commentary

Sterling Harwood

With
Without
And who'll deny
It's what the fighting's
all about.
-- Roger Waters*

I shall consider two main problems raised by Professor Ryder's thought-provoking paper. First, is Ryder's interpretation of Madison's "Federalist No. 10" correct? Second, is the Constitution, as Ryder claims, an obstacle to social progress?[1] I focus on "Federalist No. 10," rather than on Madison's account of the Constitutional Convention, on which Ryder also relies, since *The Federalist* is simply much more reliable. As Stephen Macedo observes:

> [N]o official record of the closed proceedings in Philadelphia was ever published, an incomprehensible oversight if it had been expected that future interpreters would be guided by the Framers' intentions. ... Madison's unofficial account of the convention, reconstructed from his notes, was published

> posthumously in 1840, after everyone who had attended the convention was dead [and thus unable to corroborate it].[2]

Some scholars charge "that Madison altered his notes in later life in order to support the partisan political positions he then espoused."[3] But even those who most convincingly rebut this charge admit that "the words Madison recorded could not, at a generous estimate, have amounted to more than ten percent of what was spoken."[4]

Interpreting "Federalist No. 10"

Ryder says "the Founders persistently and consistently employed a class analysis of society in general and of the proper ends of government."[5] I see, however, no persuasive evidence of class bias in "Federalist No. 10." And Charles Beard's book which purports to show the Founders' class bias, and which devotes an entire chapter to *The Federalist*, does not even once cite "Federalist No. 10."[6] I deny that, as Ryder says, the Founders *took for granted* that propertied interests should prevail over unpropertied interests.[7] Taking that for granted does not follow even if, as Ryder claims, the Founders deny that each faction's interests are equally legitimate. For the inferior interest may still be legitimate and crucial. After all, the Founders rejected all proposals to make ownership of property a constitutional requirement for the right to vote. And any inequality of the legitimacy of the interests may be entirely explained by the Founders' view, which Ryder admits is admirable, that the superior, propertied interests were, compared to the unpropertied interests, more in the interest of the common good.

Further, since Madison repeatedly expresses much concern for the common good, he cannot *consistently* take protection of property for granted, unless, perhaps, he takes for granted that protecting property is for the common good, which would not be a class bias. Ryder's interpretation imputes a major *inconsistency* to Madison, which violates the interpretive principle of charity. Since Madison values the common good, which includes the interests of the unpropertied, he is *committed* to refusing to dismiss the interests of the unpropertied. Ryder says that the most striking example of misunderstanding caused by neglecting the Founders' class analysis is thinking that the Founders believe "government is essentially an arena in which a plurality of interests and pursuits interact, and that such interaction should lead, if government is properly constituted, to the greater good of the society as a whole."[8] But I will argue that this striking example is an interpretation superior to Ryder's.

A major fear that democratic government is especially unstable and perishable pervades "Federalist No. 10." Madison apparently thought the collapse of the new American democracy would be contrary to the greater good of the society as a whole, that is, contrary to the common good. I agree with Ryder that there is a class analysis in No. 10, since Madison discusses factions, which are classes. But as we shall see, factions include many significant non-economic classes (e.g., religious factions). So Madison's class analysis is not exclusively, or even primarily, an economic class analysis. Further, since I see Madison's analysis primarily as the means intended to further the end of promoting the common good, I do not see the class analysis as a class bias. I agree with Ryder that it is a mistake to try to show a class bias by simply trying to ascribe to the Founders the individualized motives of narrow, financial self-interest.[9] Claiming that the Founders favored the propertied simply because the Founders were propertied is an *ad hominem* argument attacking the messengers rather than any class-biased message.[10]

Here is the textual evidence for my interpretation that Madison was concerned at least as much with the common or public good as he was with private property rights. Also, note that Madison was concerned with the non-economic classes as well as economic classes when he said:

> zeal for different opinions concerning religion, concerning government, and many other points . . . ; an attachment to different leaders ambitiously contending for pre-eminence and power; or to persons of other descriptions whose fortunes have been interested to the human passions, have, in turn, divided mankind into parties, inflamed them with mutual animosity, and rendered them much more disposed to vex and oppress each other than to co-operate for their *common good*.[11]

Madison also says:

> It is vain to say that enlightened statesmen will be able to adjust these clashing interests, and render them all subservient to *the public good*. Enlightened statesmen will not always be at

> the helm. Nor, in many cases, can such an adjustment be made at all without taking into view indirect and remote considerations, which will rarely prevail over the immediate interest which one party may find in disregarding the rights of another or the *good of the whole*.[12]

As Ryder notes, Madison said: "To secure the *public good* and private rights against the danger of [a majority] faction, and at the same time to preserve the spirit and the form of popular government, is then the great object to which our inquiries are directed."[13] Madison prominently considers the public good. And private rights are not limited to property rights, since they include rights to freedom of religious worship, and so forth. Further, Madison begins by claiming that his arguments are in the interest of *any* "friend of popular governments," since the "instability, injustice, and confusion introduced" by factions have "been the mortal diseases under which popular governments have everywhere perished . . . "[14] Madison tries to show how democratic government can control factions, and he assumes that the perishing of American democratic government is contrary to the common good. Madison's concern for the common good is evident even in his definition of a faction:

> a number of citizens, whether amounting to a majority or minority of the whole, who are united and actuated by some common impulse of passion, or of interest, adverse to the rights of other citizens, *or* to the permanent and aggregate interests of the *community*.[15]

Again, communal or common interests get equal time in Madison's considerations.

Madison is, of course, *also* concerned with rights to private property. But such a concern need not be a class bias. Far from it, for as Ryder notes, the Founders' "principles of economic liberalism which allowed the release of the extraordinary power of private capital . . . was to be admired."[16] It seems clearly in the common interest of people in a new, growing country to release this extraordinary power to propel growth and promote the country's development and maturation. The common good would converge with the alleged class bias for the propertied. So the common good, along with respect for Lockean property rights, both seem to motivate Madison even when he may seem to have a class bias, as when he said a "rage for . . . equal division of property" is an "improper or wicked project."[17] One need not have a class bias, or a Lockean theory of property, to condemn dividing property equally, regardless of how hard people have worked to get it. Sufficient for such a condemnation are (1) the unfair surprise of pulling the rug out from under people by taking their life's savings, and (2) the deterring of the release of the extraordinary power of private capital to raise standards of living generally. Madison's consideration of classes is best explained not by a motive of class bias, but by the understandably urgent motive of forming a union, a nation, of many classes, including economic and non-economic classes. The nation's motto even then was *E pluribus unum* -- out of many, one.

Is The Constitution An Obstacle to Social Progress?

Ryder says the principles that informed the Constitution at its inception continue to inform the Constitution in many crucial respects, and form a significant obstacle to social progress and democratic government. Is this so? Before answering "yes," Ryder must solve two problems.

First, Ryder admits his thesis that the Founders used a class analysis is:

> a minority view, and the fact that most of the literature which deals with the Constitution and the events and issues related to it has failed to appreciate and employ the Founders' own class analysis had led to serious misunderstandings of the Founders' intentions and of the new form of government they created.[18]

But if Ryder is right, why has not this great failure and misunderstanding prevented the Founders' class principles from crucially informing the Constitution and from forming a significant obstacle to social progress, as Ryder claims? Ryder seems inconsistent. Further, why should the Founders' principles crucially inform the Constitution, since, as we saw above, Macedo argues that the Founders would have kept better, official records were their original intentions and principles to be crucial?

Second, Ryder must rebut Frank Michelman's arguments that, on the contrary, the Constitution is an important source of social progress toward democratic participation and welfare rights, rights the poor have to food, shelter, clothing, education and health. The gist of Michelman's argument is:

to will the Founders' end, democratic participation, is to will the necessary means to that end, welfare rights. Michelman argues:

> Without basic education--without the literacy, fluency, and elementary understanding of politics and markets that are hard to obtain without it--what hope is there of effective participation in the last-resort political system? On just this basis, it seems, the Supreme Court itself has expressly allowed that "some identifiable quantum of education" may be a constitutional right. But if so, then what about life itself, health and vigor, presentable attire, or shelter not only from the onslaughts of social debilitation? Are not these interests the universal, rock-bottom prerequisites of effective participation in democratic representation--even paramount in importance to education and, certainly, to the niceties of apportionment, districting, and ballot access . . .? How can there be those sophisticated rights to a formally unbiased majoritarian system, but no rights to the indispensible means of effective participation in that system?[19]

Thus the Constitution, properly interpreted, promises to be a compelling force for progressive change.[20]

NOTES

* From "Us and Them," on *The Dark Side of the Moon* by Pink Floyd (Harvest Records, 1973).

1. John Ryder, "Private Property and the U.S. Constitution," p. 25.

2. Stephen Macedo, *The New Right v. The Constitution.* (CATO Institute, 1986), p. 10. See also, Winton U. Solberg, *The Federal Convention and the Formation of the Union of American States.* (Bobbs-Merrill Co., 1976), pp. 67-70.

3. Edmund S. Morgan, "Popular Fiction," *The New Republic*, June 29, 1987, p. 28.

4. *Ibid.*

5. Ryder, p. 17.

6. Charles A. Beard, *An Economic Interpretation of the Constitution of the United States.* (Macmillan, 1935, originally 1913), esp. Ch. 6. Note that Beard is quite cynical about the general good, saying: "Of course it may be shown that the 'general good' is the ostensible object of any particular act; but the general good is a passive force, and unless we know who are the several individuals that benefit in its name, it has no meaning." *Ibid.*, p. 155. But we have no reason to assume that the general good is always--or even usually -- reducible to the good of only the *special* class of individuals who actively promoted the so-called *general* good. For a general convergence of interests, and even altruism, are often known to motivate actions.

> Further, note the argument that Forrest McDonald exhaustively analyzed the economic interests not only of the members of the Philadelphia convention but also of every member of every state ratifying convention. The result was a highly complex picture that served to discredit and replace Charles Beard's simplistic *Economic Interpretation of the Constitution.*

Morgan, p. 30. See also Forrest McDonald, *We the People: The Economic Origins of the Constitution.* (University of Chicago, 1958).

7. Ryder, p. 24.

8. *Ibid.*, p. 17.

9. *Ibid.*, p. 19.

10. I call this the *ad hominem* fallacy, but others call it the genetic fallacy. See, Richard W. Miller, *Analyzing Marx.* (Princeton, 1984), p. 48f.

Frederick Engels is a striking counterexample to the arguments committing these fallacies. Engels was a member of a bourgeois family. His father was a manufacturer and Engels served in a commercial firm owned by his father. But Engels had no class bias for the bourgeoisie. On the contrary, he had a class bias for the proletariat. See, V. I. Lenin, "Frederick Engels," in *Karl Marx & Frederick Engels: Selected Works*. (International Publishers, 1968). pp. 16-17.

11. James Madison, *The Federalist Papers*, No. 10, paragraph 7, emphasis added.

12. *Ibid.*, paragraph 9, emphasis added.

13. Ryder, p. 22, quoting Madison.

14. Madison, paragraph 1.

15. *Ibid.*, paragraph 2, emphasis added.

16. Ryder, p. 25.

17. Madison, penultimate paragraph.

18. Ryder, p. 17. One explanation of why Ryder's is the minority view is the persuasiveness of the work of Forrest McDonald. See note 6, above.

19. Frank I. Michelman, "Welfare Rights In a Constitutional Democracy," 1979 *Washington University Law Quarterly* 659 (1979), p. 677.

20. Ryder gives little or no support for his claims, near the end of his paper, about the Constitution's allegedly unhelpful role in foreign policy. Of course, many invoked the Constitution to criticize those in the Iran/Contra scandal. For example, some used the metaphor of Oliver North shredding the Constitution. And there are, for example, at least plausible arguments for the unconstitutionality of America's undeclared war in Vietnam. See, e.g., Ronald Dworkin, *Taking Rights Seriously* (Harvard University Press, 1977), Ch. 8. The Constitution democratically leaves much power to the people. Ryder fails to show that the Constitution, moreso than the popular electorate, is to blame for allowing abuses of power.

THE DEBATES ON THE CONSTITUTION: PHILOSOPHICAL THEORY AND PRAXIS IN FORMULATING THE U.S. CONSTITUTION OF 1787

David Fortunoff

Professor Blau's "Government or Anarchy? (In the Debate On the Constitution)" and Professor Reck's "Philosophy in the Debates at the U.S. Constitutional Convention of 1787" present two perspectives on the function and scope of philosophical contributions to the making of the U.S. Constitution. Each title circumscribes the scope of its query to the "Debates" that attended that making, though we should note that Blau's paper ripples farther out from that focal point than Reck's, which holds its proposed center. Taking my cue from these two rhetorical structures I will direct my paper on and around their discussions.[1]

Reck begins by noting the "paucity" of the "use and mention of the philosophers during the debates" and the "meagre citations to philosophers" in the records of the debates. He judges this not to have been much enriched by the few citations of Montesquieu he finds. Reck sketches the opposite social philosophies of Hamilton and Pinckney, but focuses on the issue of sovereignty dividing Randolph and Paterson. Both adhered to the conventional doctrine that sovereignty is absolute and "integral." Through the ministrations of Franklin, the Great Compromise was wrought, and the new political principle of shared sovereignty was born.

Blau's paper, on the other hand, focuses upon meanings and implicit issues behind these broader generalizations. He sees the pivotal issue within the minds of many delegates as having been one of constitution or anarchy--as his title suggests. Blau then reviews the history of essential and antecedent distinctions in the philosophy of law between natural and national law, natural and positive law, as well as society's conflicted need for laws to be simultaneously predictable yet flexible, and to address themselves to individual's obligations as well as rights.

We can profit, it seems, from submitting Reck's narrower framework to Blau's distinction-making to yield a perspective of philosophy's more implicit influence upon the thought of the Founders. Let us proceed by observing the process of doing philosophy in the tradition of the Founders' European contemporaries and their immediate predecessors.

As we have said, both papers share a common observation that the participants at the Constitutional Convention were men "who, engaged in an historic struggle, surpassed themselves and their philosophical predecessors with the invention of a new political principle"--that is, the principle of shared sovereignty between separate states and a federal government. Furthermore, both share the suggestion that many of these men, while at their best, modified some positions they had held earlier in the Revolutionary period. John Adams, Blau tells us for example, came to disagree with the proposition that democracy required unrestrained equality. By 1787, Adams had arrived at the position--held earlier by Hamilton--that too much equality entails anarchy as much as too much inequality does tyranny. Constitutional government came to be seen as a safeguard against both. These men came to believe and argue, as Blau notes, that former appeals to *reason* must be supplanted in the Constitutional Debates by appeals to *experience*. The business of the United States' political integrity having been better assured by Revolution, now the same must be done for the business of managing and preserving it; the forces once turned toward separation must now yield to those for union.

Thus, an overriding concern in calling for the Convention was the commerce of the nation specifically, as well as other "exigencies of the Union" generally, if the new country was to rise to its challenge. These latter points were made clear by the resolutions of the Annapolis Convention, which proposed the Philadelphia Convention. But the practicality of these concerns, when compared with the idealism of a decade or so before, gives us pause to wonder whether the same revolutionaries devoted to radical separation for the purpose of founding a democracy in 1776 could a decade later also administer it. More generally posed, the question is, Can any philosophy serve both divergent needs without being self-conflicted? Yet it is perhaps less remarkable that these same men did do both than that they did so by consistently following the guiding light of the same philosophers at each occasion.

Perhaps we can achieve greater clarity in this by cutting down through the strata that lay buried beneath the citations of Montesquieu by participants in the Debates; these citations are not without a certain complexity of signification. The issue is critical, for it forms the basis of what Reck judges to be the "paucity of references" to the philosophers in the Debates. Slicing down through Montesquieu, then, we find a firm footing in the French *philosophes* for instance. In general, they were neither truly democrats nor revolutionaries, though some basic democratic principles passed though and originated from them. But democratic administration in practice is a matter different from democratic theory. Not surprisingly, then, do we find this tradition littered with revisions, renunciations, and successive philosophical overcomings: Voltaire, for example, satirized Rousseau's equalitarianism and mistrusted the people's vulnerability to "superstition and fanaticism," while still espousing the rights of man. Rousseau, in turn, while proclaiming in the "sovereignty of the people,"[2] yet mistrusted democracy and upheld the "belief that democratic administrative procedures were impossible in large nations."[3] (To this Montesquieu suggested the remedy of a "federated republic," which was an idea carried forth by Jefferson's ward system, as well as by the Unionists' position at the Convention.) But to return . . . Diderot filled much the same critical function for Helvetius' theory of equal natural endowments of men as Voltaire did for Rousseau. Montesquieu ultimately defended a principle of natural nobility. Even Jefferson, in developing his educational philosophy, acknowledged a natural inequality among men and advocated that leadership as well as education be commanded over to what he termed a "natural aristocracy of the intellect." Descartes' avowal that the innate equality of men under natural law was "antecedent to every positive and written law"[4] was formidably challenged by Gassendi and Voltaire. Finally, for both Voltaire and Diderot, too much democracy amounted to "universal license and anarchy."

To some, such oppositions, often occurring in the thought of the same philosopher, are indicative of inconsistency and paradox. Yet one feels it less so to be the case when one inclines to recall the distinctions these men insisted upon between theory and praxis. They all, surely with the utmost sincerity, sought to define, secure, protect, and defend the principles of human rights and sovereignty upon the firmest footing *for the long run*. So we learn that democracy, as an abstract concept of rights and liberties, must be modulated with regard to practice by obligation and law. As Dewey was to maintain many years later, though these concerns are connected, there is yet a "distinction between democracy as a social idea and political democracy as a system of government . . . The idea remains barren and empty save as it is incarnated in human relationships."[5]

These relationships again bring us back to Montesquieu, this time to his notion that democracy depends upon the people's sovereignty, suffrage, and management of all that is within the scope of their abilities. Continuing, he appraises the highest managerial ability of people to be the selection of those ministers who will manage governmental affairs. The relation of positive laws to these ministers is one of virtue. When virtue departs the polity, so does freedom under submission to the law. Then, men long for a different "freedom": a freedom "to act against law; and as each citizen is [then] like a slave who has run away from his master, that which was [formerly] a maxim of equity he [now] calls rigor. . . ."[6]

In this matter, what Blau reports as Adams' later "newly strengthened belief in inequality" hardly diverges from Montesquieu's thought, as Blau suggests. For we also find that Montesquieu observing that "the true spirit of equality" bears no resemblance to the condition of "extreme equality." Though he agreed with the proposition that "In the state of nature . . . all men are born equal," he also added that "they cannot continue in this equality. Society makes them lose it, and they recover it only by protection of the laws."[7] The true spirit of equality and democracy for him lay in man's submission to law; the true spirit of equality "endeavors not to shake off the authority of a master, but [only] that its masters should be none but its equals."[8]

It seems that some such idea as this must have been replicated in the minds of the Great Compromisers by virtue of a striking analogy. For, if democracy is served by the subjugation of sovereign men to their equals among men, might it not also be served by an analogous subjugation of sovereign States to their equal in the form of a federal "state" among states?

The striking similarity between the tradition of thought behind Montesquieu and the later thought of Adams and his fellow Unionists belies the notion that they surpassed their philosophical predecessors. Rather, it speaks for the counter alternative that what they surpassed and supplanted was only their own partial understanding of them. Rising to the challenge of the Convention, then, was for them a function of their changed interests and shifted perspective on the past to accommodate the future.

NOTES

1. Joseph L. Blau, "Government or Anarchy? (In the Debate on the Constitution)," *Transactions of the Charles S. Peirce Society* 23.4 (1987); and Andrew J. Reck, "Philosophy in the Debates at the U.S. Constitutional Convention of 1787," in *Philosophical Perspectives on the Constitution*, ed., Allen Rosenbaum. (Greenwood Press, 1988).

2. Norman L. Torrey, ed., *Les Philosophes*. (New York: G.P. Putnam's Sons, 1960), p. 18.

3. *Ibid.*, p. 19.

4. *Ibid.*

5. John Dewey, *The Public and Its Problems*. (Athens, Ohio: Ohio University Press, 1985), p. 143.

6. Torrey, p. 96.

7. *Ibid.*, p. 99.

8. *Ibid.*

FREEDOM OF RELIGION:
A FAILURE OF AMERICAN PHILOSOPHY

John Waide

Freedom of religion, under a common interpretation of the First Amendment of the Constitution, is a mistaken and confused ideal. Against a prominent conservative attack on the usual interpretation, a different interpretation yields consequences similar to those of Supreme Court majority opinions of the last few decades. The failure to develop a consensus for a new interpretation is a failure of American philosophy, one that I hope we will be able to rectify.

I

The first amendment to the Constitution begins "Congress shall make no law respecting an establishment of religion, or prohibiting the free exercise thereof . . . " I shall argue that this language, as usually interpreted, is incoherent. In brief, any adequately broad definition of religion for purposes of the free exercise clause will be so inclusive as to make conflict between religion and government inevitable for the purposes of the establishment clause. To show how this conflict arises, it is necessary to look briefly at what may be called the usual interpretation of these two clauses.

The usual interpretation may be summed up in the following "established principle" of judicial interpretation and constitutional law: "Government must pursue a course of complete neutrality toward religion."[1] This guiding principle shapes the interpretation of some of the key terms in the first amendment. Congress and, since the 14th amendment,[2] the states may make no law establishing a religion. But what does "establish" mean? Complete neutrality requires not only that there be no official state religion comparable to what is found in Great Britain, but that there be no support given to any religion against others, or even against the option of no religious commitment.[3] In Thomas Jefferson's oft-quoted words, the establishment clause erects "a wall of separation between church and State."[4] In the case of the free exercise clause too, neutrality is the guiding theme. As early as 1872 a court articulated this standard:

> The great bulk of human affairs and human interests is left by any free government to individual enterprise and individual action. Religion is eminently one of these interests, lying outside the true and legitimate providence of government.[5]

Accordingly, religious practice or belief is to be neither proscribed nor prescribed by government.

But what is religion? What is a religious organization, belief or practice? If we adopt James Madison's 1784 definition of religion as "the duty which we owe to our creator, and the manner of discharging it,"[6] we will eliminate all non-theistic religions and forms of religious practice. In fact, the Supreme Court has gradually broadened its definition of "religion" in response to developments in the academic study of religion. Bowser offers the following summary of the court's present view:

> that is religious which is related by doctrinal, ethical or ritualistic consideration to the Ultimate Concern (identified as God, Nature, Humanity or other) in the life of an individual or group, the belief or faith to which all else is subordinate and which occupies in the life of its possessor a place parallel to that filled by the orthodox belief in God, giving fundamental meaning to life and dictating standards of belief, conduct or worship.[7]

Under this formula, one need not be a theist or even a member of an organization to qualify for protection under the first amendment.

The free exercise clause requires such a broad functional definition of religion, otherwise the government becomes an arbiter of orthodoxy. Under current interpretations, the courts can inquire only into the sincerity of a person's belief and its place in his or her life, not the truth or falsity of a putative religious belief. As a consequence, one who denies the existence of a deity but believes deeply in and tries to live in accord with certain moral principles might well come under the protection of the first amendment and gain conscientious objector status, if a pacifist, or complain of the content of a public school textbook as a violation of his or her religion.[8]

The establishment clause, if it uses the same definition of religion that has developed mainly in response to the free exercise clause, brings religion inexorably in conflict with the concerns of government. In particular, if we consider secular humanism a religion, then it will be quite difficult for government to remain neutral concerning religion. To see this clearly, we should look at the court's current test for use in establishment clause cases.

In Lemon v. Kurtzman the court articulated the so-called Lemon standard, a three-pronged test for constitutional infirmity:

> First, the statute must have a secular legislative purpose; second, its principal or primary effect must be one that neither advances not inhibits religion, . . .; finally, the statute must not foster "an excessive government entanglement with religion."[9]

A statute must pass all three tests in order to be constitutional. If the constitution requires that statutes have a secular purpose, and yet secular humanism is a religion, then a statute with a secular purpose might further the purposes of a particular religion. But matters get worse with the second prong. It is difficult to determine the principal or primary effect of a statute. From whose point of view are we to judge the principal or primary effect? From the point of view of the state, a compulsory education law has neither a principal nor a primary effect of advancing or inhibiting religion. Its main effects concern kids who want to leave school for other reasons. But from the point of view of someone of an unorthodox and comprehensive religion, as for instance the Amish litigants in *Wisconsin v. Yoder*,[10] the principal or primary effect is indeed to inhibit their religion.

The full extent of the conflict will be most apparent if we imagine ourselves as prototypical East Tennessee fundamentalist Protestant Christians. To do so is difficult and unpleasant for me, but let us do so anyway. We find that almost every exhibit in the Smithsonian Museum of Natural History either teaches or assumes that evolutionary theory is correct and that our religious beliefs are wrong. Federal funds for biological research and education are allocated as though our creationist beliefs are false. Much of the government is devoted to furthering a commercial hedonism that our religious tradition teaches us is sinful. Alcoholic beverages are served at many government functions. In short, it might seem that many government actions and policies constitute an endorsement of the secular humanist religion. Given these affronts to our faith, who can be surprised by the energy with which we condemn secular humanism? Small consolation would we derive from the phrases "under God" in the Pledge of Allegiance and "In God We Trust" on the coins; still less from knowing that Congress opens its sessions with prayers. We could conduct a reverse thought experiment imagining ourselves as secular humanists, with similarly offensive results.

How can a government in our society remain utterly neutral between the fundamentalist and the secular humanist? If religion is to be defined broadly enough to include secular humanism, then much of what government does which could otherwise be interpreted as not getting involved in religion, becomes an endorsement of a particular religious view. That most of us practice a domesticated, neutered religion which asks that we do little that would take us out of our way or inconvenience us does not mean that more vital, ardent religious traditions will not challenge the established order of things, including much of what we regard as the province of government. The whole project of government neutrality on religion is misguided, a mistaken and confused ideal. It is based on the assumption that the scope of religion and the scope of government do not overlap, that the "true and legitimate province of government" is utterly distinct from the true and legitimate province of religion. If we take seriously either government or religion, however, the two must necessarily overlap. There is the conflict.

One proposed repair is worth a brief discussion. Following Dewey's distinction between religion and the religious,[11] Boyan has suggested that the court should adopt an *institutional* definition of religion for purposes of the establishment clause and an *operational* definition for purposes of the free exercise clause.[12] This would permit narrowing the definition in the establishment clause to avoid conflicts like those above. An approach like this, however, seems to do excessive violence to the text of the Constitution and the language of the amendment.[13]

The heart of the conflict I have described lies in the assumption that the scope of religion and the scope of government do not overlap. They do, though their territories are not entirely coextensive. And it is not due to some imperialistic tendencies of either. This conflict, however, may not arise if we restrict our definition of religion. That, however, would be a mistake, though I will not argue the point here. I will now turn to a recent influential proposal that we avoid the conflict by reinterpreting the First Amendment.

II

Chief Justice William Rehnquist has criticized recent freedom of religion decisions and has set out his objections in a comprehensive way in his dissenting opinion in *Wallace v. Jaffree*.[14] His arguments against the direction and analysis employed by the court majority are (1) the intent of the founders was not to protect what the court now tries to protect, and (2) the court's decisions over the past few decades are inconsistent and make no sense, in part because the Lemon standard is vague.[15] Each of these arguments is important and interesting.

(1) Rehnquist gives a summary of the history of the religion clause of the First Amendment.[16] His historical account may be influential,[17] so we should look at it closely. Here, however, I must be brief. His conclusion is the following:

> The Framers intended the Establishment Clause to prohibit the designation of any church as a "national" one. The Clause was also designed to stop the Federal Government from asserting a preference for one religious denomination or sect over others. . . . As its history abundantly shows, however,

> nothing in the Establishment Clause requires government to be strictly neutral between religion and irreligion . . .[18]

In other words, Rehnquist interprets the establishment clause as though it said "Congress shall make no law establishing one religious sect or society in preference to others." This exact language, however, was voted *down* by the Senate in September 1789[19] -- a fact Rehnquist omits from his otherwise detailed account of the history of the amendment.[20] Precisely the interpretation that Rehnquist imputes to the framers was considered and rejected by them.[21]

(2) Rehnquist argues that judgments formed by the theory of government neutrality and rigid separation from religion have been "neither principled nor unified."[22] The wall of separation, he contends, is "merely a 'blurred, indistinct, and variable barrier,' which 'is not wholly accurate' and can only be 'dimly perceived'."[23] He goes on to list decisions which seem, at least on his account, to draw arbitrary lines. His suggestion is that if the guidelines of the court marked an important distinction, they would not look so arbitrary, forbidding one activity and permitting an almost identical activity.

Here I believe Rehnquist commits an error which it is far beyond the scope of this paper to correct. The fact that a distinction does not mark an obvious and clear difference at its border does not show us that it is clearly a mistake.[24] In fact, we should be surprised if decisions under the First Amendment seemed obvious. There are people in this country who want a government-endorsed religion.[25] When there are people using their considerable ingenuity to test a line you have drawn for good reasons, the result is almost always that your line will be made to seem arbitrary. Most parents, for instance, learn this lesson because of their children.

Rehnquist's arguments are not persuasive, but his first argument makes an important point. Conservatives are right to insist on fidelity to the intent of the framers, so far as that can be known, in the interests of continuity. But here, we should stand back from the details of their intent, details which were necessarily shaped by their own circumstances, experiences, and limited foresight. The most urgent concern of the framers was that no national religion be established as in Great Britain. They could, however, have stated that quite simply. It is evident from the various forms of the first amendment that were considered that there was interest in going beyond simply prohibiting a national religion. Furthermore, they may have appreciated that there may be many degrees of establishment. These they left to each generation to decide upon. Finally, it is clear that the issue itself was divisive and that there was no consensus concerning the practice to be followed. The day after the House of Representatives adopted the language of the First Amendment religion clause, it voted (though not without dissent) to ask the president to proclaim a day of Thanksgiving to "Almighty God." Almost every president since (Thomas Jefferson is one clear exception) has issued such a proclamation.[26] In light of these difficulties, it should be especially clear that we need to step back from the framers' proximate intentions to their broader intentions.

It would be most helpful to ask what was the chief evil that framers intended to prevent.[27] These chief evils seem clearly, even to Rehnquist's sources on the subject, to have been "religious persecution" and "subversion of the rights of conscience in matters of religion."[28] That some of them, at least Thomas Jefferson, had a broader and more positive ideal of religious freedom also seems clear. It is the negative purpose, however, that is most informative here and which may easily give us a connection between the framers' intent and applications to recent problems they could not have foreseen. If we are chiefly concerned to prevent religious persecution and subversion of conscience, then the lines the court has followed in its free exercise cases are more or less correct.[29] Not to allow, for example, for conscientious objectors to military service would be a violation of conscience and to imprison faithful pacifists would be a form of persecution. Similarly, concerning the establishment clause, to permit public schools to require or encourage prayer in a way that would set apart those whose beliefs do not conform to the prevailing majority is to promote the conditions for religious persecution in the elementary schools.

Though I have only hinted at it, we have a way of construing the language of the first amendment so as to preserve the framers' intent and bring it into continuity with decisions concerning problems they could not have foreseen. Even this interpretation, however, does not fully remove the conflicts which arise from the expanded definition of religion. Given my remarks above, both the fundamentalist and the atheist will feel persecuted to some degree in our present society. My attempt here, has been to argue against an interpretation that would make things considerably worse than at present and offer an alternative which responds to the legitimate concern for continuity, though without extricating us from the conflict I developed in section one.

III

I will close by suggesting, though much too briefly, that our present conflict is at least partly a result of a failure of American philosophy. In short, my criticism is that American philosophy since William James, has not taken religion seriously as an element in public life. The models of public dialogue--Dewey's method of intelligence is the most prominent example--omit religious traditions as participants. Part of the result has been that we do not have a coherent and applicable method of public dialogue in matters concerning religion. Since religion overlaps so much of public life, this means fruitful public dialogue is, at best, rare.

American philosophy played an important role in expanding the definition of religion, one of the steps to our present conflict.[30] American philosophers, however, have not been able to articulate and put into practice methods of bringing religion into the public arena in any constructive way. I will focus my critique on Dewey because he was the most influential of our public philosophers and his failure was greatest.

The experimental method, the method of intelligence--Dewey used different terms at different times--never included religious traditions, their symbols, their stories, their rituals. These were omitted entirely from most of Dewey's writings. At the age of 75, he finally faced religion squarely in *A Common Faith*. There he argued that

> The opposition between religious values as I conceive them and religions is not to be bridged. Just because the release of these values is so important, their identification with the creeds and cults of religions must be dissolved.[31]

In short, although Dewey saw important values embodied in religious experience, he believed that what is valuable in religion can be separated from creeds and cults--which I take to mean the symbols, stories, and rituals of specific religious traditions and communities--and promoted in purity apart from those traditions and communities. This strikes me as a serious error, though now is not the time to pursue that issue.[32]

Dewey did not see much value in religion as practiced by particular communities. It is hardly surprising, then, that he did not engage in much dialogue with representatives of those communities. Dewey visited schools, not churches. Who, then, should be surprised that his theory of public policy dialogue did not include religious communities and traditions as participants?

If we are to be able to articulate and practice a coherent ideal of religious freedom, I believe it will have to include a model of public dialogue that includes religious communities and traditions--their symbols, stories, and rituals. Is such a dialogue possible? What legal or self-imposed restraints--upon government, upon religious communities, upon individuals--are required for such dialogue to be fruitful? These are important questions we have yet to answer. But there are others. I have assumed that religion has more and different value than Dewey argued. But is this correct? Even if the value of religion is different, are religions something to be overcome, as Dewey seemed to think, or something to be integrated into the public dialogue of the community. If the latter, how can we do it? How might such dialogue change religious communities as well as public policy discussion? Can freedom of religion be preserved in public dialogue that includes religious communities and traditions?

We do not yet have answers to these questions, though there are a few encouraging signs. Fontinell's *Toward a Reconstruction of Religion*[33] is a small step toward a public dialogue that explicitly tries to build on pragmatist insights. More recently, Bellah[34] and Sullivan[35] have begun to put forward proposals for the importance of religion as an element in public philosophy and public discourse. We can only work and wait for these lines of inquiry to bear fruit.[36] If they do not, it seems to me that religious freedom is in a mess.

CONCLUSION

I have argued that an appropriately expansive definition of 'religion' for the purposes of the free exercise clause brings the state inexorably in conflict with religion under the establishment clause. I have criticized Rehnquist's proposed contraction of the scope of the first amendment while trying to preserve his insistence on fidelity to the intent of the framers. Finally, I have suggested that American philosophy has failed to enter into dialogue with religious traditions and to articulate models of public policy dialogue that would permit the participation of religious communities. I suggest that freedom of religion must finally be understood and put into practice through public dialogue that affirms the value and participation of religious communities.

NOTES

1. *Wallace v. Jaffree* 105 S.Ct. 2492 (1985), Justice Stevens writing for the majority. He cites several decisions to support his claim that this is an established principle.

2. See Michael Ken Curtis, *No State Shall Abridge: The Fourteenth Amendment and the Bill of Rights.* (Durham, NC: Duke University Press, 1986). The conventional interpretation of the 14th amendment has lately been attacked by conservatives--most notably Attorney General Edwin Meese. Curtis defends on historical grounds the view that the fourteenth amendment protects the liberties outlined in the Bill of Rights from state as well as federal violation.

3. "The 'establishment of religion' clause of the First Amendment means at least this: Neither a state nor the Federal Government can set up a church. Neither can pass laws which aid one religion, aid all religions, or prefer one religion over another." *Everson v. Board of Education* 330 U.S. 15 (1947). Quoted in A. Stephen Boyan, Jr., "Defining Religion in Operational and Institutional Terms," *University of Pennsylvania Law Review* 116 (1968)480.

4. Quoted by Rehnquist, *Wallace v. Jaffree* 105 S.Ct. 2509 (1985).

5. *Board of Education v. Minor*, 23 Ohio St. 211, 253, quoted approvingly in *Abington School District v. Schempp*, 374 U.S. 203, 215, n. 7, 83 S.Ct. 1560, 1567, no. 7, 10, L.Ed. 2d 844 (1963).

6. Madison, "A Memorial and Remonstrance on the Religious Rights of Man," in *Cornerstones of Religious Freedom in America.* p. 84 (J. Blau, ed., 1964); cited in Boyan, p. 483.

7. Anita Bowser, "Delimiting Religion in the Constitution: A Classification Problem," *Valparaiso University Law Review* 11 (1977)225-226.

8. Even with the expansive definition, however, the court has been reluctant to protect inconvenient religious practices, as opposed to religious beliefs. Polygamy, frequent holy days requiring abstinence from work, prohibitions on certain kinds of medical treatment and other religious practices which go beyond the bounds of domesticated religion in the U.S.A. do not necessarily receive protection. As soon as we include under 'religion' unorthodox public practices, as opposed to private belief and ritual, religious freedom seems unavailable. As Stanley Hauerwas has observed in "Freedom of Religion: A Subtle Temptation" (unpublished, final footnote), it would be more accurate to call our policy, "tolerance of religion" rather than freedom of religion." Still, these are not the conflicts which make the ideal of freedom of religion, understood as neutrality, an incoherent ideal.

9. *Lemon v. Kurtzman*, 403 U.S. 602, 612-13, 91 S.Ct. 2105, 2111, 29 L.Ed. 2d 745 (1971); quoted in *Wallace v. Jaffree* 105 S.Ct. 2489 (1985).

10. 406 U.S. 203 (1972); cited in Bowser, p. 219, n. 297.

11. John Dewey, *A Common Faith*. (New Haven: Yale University Press, 1934).

12. A. Stephen Boyan, Jr., "Defining Religion in Operational and Institutional Terms," *University of Pennsylvania Law Review* 116 (1968)479-498. For a similar approach, see also "Note: Towards a Constitutional Definition of Religion," *Harvard Law Review* 91 (1978)1056-1089

13. " 'Religion' appears only once in the [First] Amendment. But the word governs two prohibitions and governs them alike. It does not have two meanings, one narrow to forbid 'an establishment' and another, much broader, for securing 'the free exercise thereof.' 'Thereof' brings down 'religion' with its entire and exact content, no more and no less, from the first into the second guaranty, so that Congress and now the states are as broadly restricted concerning the one as they are regarding the other." *Everson v. Board of Education* 330 U.S. 1, 32 (1947), Rutledge, dissenting; cited in "Note: Toward a Constitutional Definition of Religion," *Harvard Law Review* 91 (1978)1085.

14. 105 S.Ct. 2508-2520 (1985).

15. Justice O'Connor advances a third argument against the tendencies of the court, though she concurs with the majority in *Wallace v. Jaffree*: (3) state legislatures should be presumed to have constitutionally permissible purposes for statutes unless there is convincing evidence to the contrary. In effect, the court, she argues, should consider a legislature innocent of impermissible purposes until proven guilty. "Even if the text and official history of a statute express no secular purpose, the statute should be held to have an improper purpose only if it is beyond purview that endorsement of religion or a religious belief 'was and is the law's reason for existence.' " (O'Connor, concurring in *Wallace v. Jaffree* 105 S.Ct. 2500). In her view, however, the Alabama statute in question in that case was definitely infirm on this point. "However deferentially one examines its text and legislative history, however objectively one views the message attempted to be conveyed to the public, the conclusion is unavoidable that the purpose of the statute is to endorse prayer in public schools." (2501) Both Burger and White, however, dissent from the majority opinion in part because they do not believe the evidence shows clearly that the purpose of the statute is to endorse prayer in public schools. This principle of deference to state legislatures is quite important and could serve to place severe and strange limits on freedom of religion, especially when interpreted by people like White, Burger, and Rehnquist.

16. *Wallace v. Jaffree* 105 S.Ct. 2508-2517 (1985).

17. "I appreciate Justice Rehnquist's explication of the history of the religion clauses of the First Amendment. Against that history, it would be quite understandable if we undertook to reassess our cases dealing with these

clauses, particularly those dealing with the Establishment Clause." *Wallace v. Jaffree* 105 S.Ct. 2508 (1985), Justice White, dissenting. Furthermore, Rehnquist is now Chief Justice.

18. *Wallace v. Jaffree* 105 S.Ct. 2520 (1985), Rehnquist, dissenting.

19. Bernard Schwartz, *The Roots of the Bill of Rights.* (New York: Chelsea House Publishers, 1971), p. 1148. Leonard W. Levy also discusses this point in *The Establishment Clause: Religion and the First Amendment.* (New York: Macmillan Publishing Company, 1986), pp. 81-82.

20. That Rehnquist omits this fact after devoting so much time to quoting debate in the House of Representatives could lead one to question the motives and honesty of his historical account. I do. Robert L. Cord, in *Separation of Church and State: Historical Fact and Current Fiction.* (New York: Lambeth Press, 1982) mentions but passes over (pp. 8-9) this obvious problem with his interpretation (which is in agreement with Rehnquist).

21. Robert Heard, "Rehnquist and the Right Not To Believe," *Texas Observer* 10 October 1986, p. 24.

22. *Wallace* 2516, Rehnquist, dissenting.

23. *Wallace* 2516-2517, Rehnquist dissenting. He cites four cases from which the phrases above come.

24. Dewey says of classification: ". . . the purpose is to facilitate our dealings with unique individuals and changing events. When we assume that our clefts and bunches represent fixed separations and collections *in rerum natura*, we obstruct rather than aid our transactions with things." John Dewey, *Human Nature and Conduct.* (New York: Random House, 1930 (1922), p. 124.

25. According to W. A. Criswell, pastor of First Baptist Church of Dallas (the largest Baptist church in the world), "This thing about separation of church and state is the figment of some infidel's imagination." Pat Robertson, a television preacher and a candidate for President in 1988, has said, "The Constitution of the United States is a marvelous document for self-government by Christian people. But the minute you turn the document into the hands of non-Christian people and atheist people, they can use it to destroy the very foundation of our society." These quotations are included in Robert Heard, "Rehnquist and the Right Not to Believe," *Texas Observer* 10 October 1986, p. 23. For another example, Alabama State Senator Donald G. Holmes, sponsor of that state's statute requiring teachers in public schools or universities to lead willing students in a prescribed prayer, is not alone in wanting to move toward state encouragement of prayer in public schools. (Alabama Code, section 16-1-20.2 (Supp. 1984). For the most part, *Wallace v. Jaffree* concerns the Alabama Code section 16-1-20.1 which required a moment of silence for meditation or prayer.)

26. *Wallace* 2513-2514, Rehnquist, dissenting.

27. Here I am consciously echoing the "cruelty first" strategy followed by Montaigne and explained so lucidly by Judith N. Schlar, *Ordinary Vices.* (Harvard University Press, 1984), pp. 7-44.

28. This phrase comes from Joseph Story (member of the Supreme Court 1811-1845), *Commentaries on the Constitution of the United States*, (5th edition, 1891). Volume 2, p. 631-632; cited by Rehnquist in *Wallace* 2515.

29. After I wrote this section, *All Things Considered* broadcast (28 January 1987) an interview: National Public Radio legal affairs correspondent Nina Totenberg conducted with Justice Brennen in which he made much of the same appeal to what I am calling the "cruelty first" argument.

30. I am thinking especially of William James' *Varieties of Religious Experience* and Dewey's distinction between "religion" and "the religious" in a *A Common Faith*. Such theologians as Paul Tillich, of course, were also important.

31. John Dewey, *A Common Faith*, p. 28.

32. If I could pursue that argument here I would draw heavily on the thought of Stanley Hauerwas as found in such books as *Truthfulness and Tragedy*. (University of Notre Dame Press, 1977); *A Community of Character*. (University of Notre Dame Press, 1981); and *The Peaceable Kingdom*. (University of Notre Dame Press, 1983).

33. Eugene Fontinell, *Toward a Reconstruction of Religion*. (New York: Doubleday and Co., 1970).

34. See especially Robert N. Bellah, Richard Madsen, William M. Sullivan, Ann Swindler, and Steven M. Tipton, *Habits of the Heart: Individualism and Commitment in American Life*. (Berkeley: University of California Press, 1985).

35. William M. Sullivan, *Reconstructing Public Philosophy*. (Berkeley: University of California Press, 1982).

36. Stanley Hauerwas' unpublished paper, "Freedom of Religion: A Subtle Temptation" has recently persuaded me that the avenues Bellah and Sullivan are exploring are less promising that I had earlier supposed.

TWO VIEWS ON THE NATURE OF RELIGIOUS COMMUNITIES: A REPLY TO WAIDE

A Commentary

Edward S. Petry, Jr.

District Judge Hand wrote that "for purposes of the First Amendment, secular humanism is a religious belief system, entitled to the protections of, and subject to the prohibitions of, the religion clauses of the U.S. Constitution." I agree with Professor Waide that this is a topic that needs to be discussed again. The topic is: the nature of the religious community, its scope and defining characteristics.

Professor Waide has raised this issue in terms of the First Amendment. He has persuasively argued that with respect to the free exercise clause, the idea of the religious community has been interpreted so broadly that it now includes secular humanists, fundamentalists and even atheists. Such a broad interpretation of a religious community actually equates a religious community with any community of persons who have sincere beliefs and demonstrate their sincerity by their actions and the established conduct of their lives. A supernatural correlate to their beliefs and even the hypothesis of God's reality are deemed to be unnecessary. This is the current standard of the court. Professor Waide is correct when he argues that this broad interpretation inevitably generates a Constitutional problem, for if government functions at all, its activities will unavoidably conflict with the sincere beliefs and actions of some persons while corresponding to those of others. But then government violates both the establishment and the free exercise clauses.

Professor Waide's solution to this dilemma is to call for a reevaluation of the ideal of a religious community and he calls on the courts and on American philosophy to participate in this reevaluation.

Professor Waide's paper demonstrates that a broad interpretation of the idea of a religious community is Constitutionally problematic. I will argue that American philosophy has offered an interpretation of the religious community that though different from the ones presented by Professor Waide is equally broad if not more so. Does this mean that the idea of a religious community in American philosophy is Constitutionally problematic? Undoubtedly; but as Plato knew so well, philosophy and politics inevitably collide, the philosopher-king fails, the man who returns to the cave is killed and Socrates drank hemlock. Philosophy cannot be adequately measured by political necessities. The Constitution is based on philosophical assumptions and as Professor Waide has shown, interpretations of it raise interesting philosophical issues, but the Constitution cannot be the measure for insuing philosophical discourse. The First Amendment only limits what the government may do respecting religion. If the court were to interpret the idea of religious community in the broad way that Charles Peirce did for instance, the government would inevitably violate both clauses of the First Amendment. But I don't believe this was a consideration for Peirce and I don't believe it should be a consideration for us in our attempts to discuss the nature of religious communities. A study of the Constitution has brought the issue to our attention but our philosophic discussion must now go beyond the Constitutional issues.

I will now focus on one direction that such a discussion of religious communities might take. In particular, I will attempt to expand on suggestions made by Professor Waide, which I believe are akin to the views of Stanley Hauerwas. I will contrast these views with those of Charles Peirce who I believe best represents an important opposing viewpoint. But before I turn to this, let me first state the basis for my general agreement with Professor Waide.

The founders of American philosophy were deeply religious men and commitments to religious communities played a central role in their philosophies. Everyone acknowledges this with respect to early American philosophers: e.g., Cotton Mather, Samuel Johnson, Jonathan Edwards, et al. All too often, however, the religious dimension of "classical," nineteenth century American philosophy and the importance of the religious community to pragmatism for instance, has been neglected. There are many reasons for this, foremost among them has been the influence of William James. James emphasized personal religious experiences. He believed that social expressions of religion through a religious community were merely conventional and were at best religion at "second hand." Along these lines John Smith has noted that "Royce pointed out many years ago [that] it is lamentable that America's most renowned philosopher and psychologist of religion, William James, should have confined his attention solely to what he regarded as personal religion. . . ."[1] On this basis, I agree with Professor Waide that contemporary American philosophy "since William James, has not taken religion seriously as an element of public life."

My agreement on this point notwithstanding, I do not believe that this constitutes a failure of American philosophy for on this particular issue James is not representative of the history of American philosophy. He is not even representative of the "classical," post-Darwinian era. Peirce, Royce, Santayana and even Dewey all differed with James. They emphasized the social dimension of religion. Professor Waide acknowledges this at least with respect to Dewey, but he still argues that in its dealings with the idea of the religious community American philosophy has failed.

This failure, as I believe Professor Waide sees it, lies in the way American philosophy has dealt with the social dimension of religion. In conclusion I would like to consider two distinct views regarding the nature of the religious community.

On the one hand, Royce, Peirce and Dewey argued for a broad, universal religious community that is not confined to any established religious tradition, sect, class or creed. Professor Waide, on the other hand, argues that any broad interpretation of the idea of a religious community commits a "serious error." In section three, he states that the idea of a religious community must include "symbols, stories and rituals of *specific* religious traditions" (my emphasis). And, in the same section, Professor Waide states that Dewey was wrong to think that "what is valuable in religion can be separated from creeds and cults." These are the two contrasting views that we must now consider in more detail.

In a footnote Professor Waide refers us to the works of Stanley Hauerwas. Throughout the text of the paper references are made to ideas that are very similar to those expressed by Hauerwas and this is especially true whenever Professor Waide suggests his own ideal of a religious community.

In the article, "On Keeping Theological Ethics Theological,"[2] Stanley Hauerwas argues for "the formation of a community distinct from the world." This community or church "embodies the stories, the rituals and others [that is, persons who are in a like manner] committed to worshipping God." Hauerwas' intention is not exclusivity as an end in itself, but rather he hopes to counter what he sees as the prevailing tendency to transform Christian ethics into just "another form of meta-ethics" or just "another system of beliefs." Hauerwas believes that these consequences can best be avoided and the power of Christianity best brought into the world, through the agency of a distinctive church "i.e., a body of people who stand apart from the 'world' because of the peculiar task of worshipping a God whom the world knows not."

This view contrasts with that of Charles Peirce. I have chosen Peirce instead of Dewey for two reasons. Religion and religious communities play a central role in Peirce's philosophy. This is not the case with Dewey. And second, I believe the contrasting views of Hauerwas and Peirce are more amenable to discussion and synthesis than are the contrasting views of Hauerwas and Dewey.

First we should note the importance that Peirce gave to religious experience and the religious community. The nature of Peirce's philosophy makes this difficult, but one of the more interesting entry-points into the problem is Peirce's comments on what he called "musement" (6.452-6.565).[3]

For Peirce, "musement" could be part of a religious experience that leads into scientific or pragmatic reasoning (6.452-6.493). The free play of thought suggests to "the muser" that seemingly disparate elements of the Universe are actually part of a conspiracy of unity (6.465). Peirce adds that "this is a specimen of certain lines of reflection which will inevitably suggest the hypothesis of God's Reality" (6.465). And further, this hypothesis supplies "the muser" with "an ideal of life" (6.465 and 8.262) and can serve as "the First Stage of scientific inquiry" and mark the beginning of "self-controlled," "pragmantistic" reasoning (5.478-6.481). Peirce associated controlled reasoning with the Christian ideal of agapastic love (2.654 and 5.339n.) and it is against this backdrop that we can understand Peirce's claim that "religious adoration" and its "consequent effects upon conduct," are essential for "good sound solid strong pragmatism [sic]" (8.262).

But, according to Peirce, it is impossible for "the muser" to develop his initial insight into either a way of life or a path or inquiry unless he participates in a community. And, consistent with Peirce's synechism," or his doctrine of continuity, and consistent with his understanding of agapism, the community must be thought of as being boundless and continually open to the possibility of new members. According to Peirce, a "little exclusive church is almost worse than none. A great catholic church is wanted" (6.443). Peirce has the following to say about distinct Christian churches and their various traditions, creeds or platforms:

> . . . whether it be that of Trent, Lambeth, Geneva, or what, there is not one plank in it that has not, as a matter of historical fact, been inserted with a view of proclaiming the damnation and of procuring the persecution of some body of convinced Christians. Hence it is that the central doctrine of love is not to be found in any one of them. (6.450).

Finally, we should note that Peirce believed that all reasonable men, not only Christians, would be instinctively drawn to his idea of a universal religious community for, as I have mentioned, Peirce believed that Christianity rests not on a creed or history or a people but on a principle that operates in all of our lives and throughout the cosmos: agapism.

It has been argued that Peirce was naive when he called for a return to the "simple gospel of Jesus" to love one's neighbor. For as John Smith has noted, many of the divisions among the churches stem from their attempts to interpret what this "simple gospel" means.[4] And further, reasonable men have had doubts about the cosmological significance of *agape*. These criticisms notwithstanding, Peirce's "ecumenical" position does present us with a contrasting perspective.

In sum, Professor Waide has shown us the need for a reevaluation of our idea of the religious community. In the past American philosophy has presented a broad, universal interpretation of the idea. Lately, contemporary American philosophy has neglected the issue almost altogether. The recent neglect and the previous broad interpretations constitute what Professor Waide has called a failure of American philosophy. In his paper, Professor Waide has suggested an alternative interpretation which contrasts with the broad interpretation of "classical" American philosophy. Though there are differences there is common ground, a common interest and a pressing need. The nature of the religious community, its scope and defining characteristics must again be recognized as vitally important topics.

NOTES

1. John E. Smith, "Religion and Theology in Peirce," P. Wiener and F. H. Young (eds.), *Studies in the Philosophy of Charles Sanders Peirce*. (Cambridge MA, 1952), p. 258.

2. Stanley Hauerwas, "On Keeping Theological Ethics Theological," S. Hauerwas and A. MacIntyre (eds.), *Revisions: Changing Perspectives in Moral Philosophy*. (Notre Dame, 1983), pp. 16-42.

3. Smith, p. 258.

4. See p. 6

CONSTITUTIONAL SECULARITY AND THE DENIAL OF RELIGIOUS FREEDOM

Michael Eldridge

The religious right and neo-conservatives have raised interesting challenges to current Constitutional interpretation and educational practice. In this paper I deal with the implications of the Constitution's secular orientation for religious freedom and our common practice. Along the way, I respond to the ill-informed, perhaps even slanderous attack on John Dewey that is being made not only by the religious right but by many academics from prestigious institutions. For them Dewey is the intellectual father of the sectarian secularism which the religious right, in particular, sees in the public schools.

Secularity and the Constitution

The Constitution is clearly a secular document. The preamble, which declares the purpose of the framers, lists several this-worldly objectives: "form a more perfect Union, establish Justice, insure domestic Tranquility, provide for the common defence, promote the general Welfare, and secure the Blessings of Liberty." Indeed, the only mention of religion is a negative one. There is a prohibition against religious tests for holding public office (Article VI, Section 3). This is no accidental secularity. The framers were devising a system of government that would enable people of the United States to secure a better life in this world for themselves. This secularity is not, however, anti-religious. Although religious tests could not be imposed on those who held public office, there is no suggestion of anti-religious sentiment. In fact, the first amendment guaranteed religious freedom. Rather, the Constitution as amended reflected a consensus that the various religions could be freely practiced, but no one of which was to dominate. Thus a public space free of religious influence was created.

We must recognize, of course, that some states had established religions. Not all government was to govern without reference to the supernatural. The first amendment reads, in part, "Congress shall make no law respecting an establishment of religion." If there had been no established religions in any of the states, this clause could have been less circumspect, reading, "Congress shall make no law establishing a religion." But the Constitutional Convention did not have a free hand. Many held diverse opinions about religion and its role in government and public life. Nevertheless, a consensus was reached that permitted the national government to concern itself with this world and leave the concern for any other world and its influence through the various sects with those religious groups.

The eighteenth century prohibition against Congressional establishment of religion, however, has been applied by the Supreme Court in the twentieth century against the state legislatures as well. Through its interpretation of the fourteenth amendment the Court has ruled in several cases that no legislation, federal or otherwise, shall have a religious purpose or effect. This extension of the no establishment clause has led to a steady erosion of religious influence, particularly in the public schools. Prayers, Bible readings and the posting of the Ten Commandments, which were all once the practice have now been banned from the classroom.

Dewey and Sectarian Secularism

The Christian right is now angrily reacting to this situation, claiming that America's schools no longer foster Christianity and indeed have been taken over by secular humanism. Moreover, they regard John Dewey as the chief spokesman for this humanism and hold him responsible for the destruction of Christian America's public schools.[1] In his statement regarding his possible presidential candidacy, Pat Robertson declared, "We have taken the Holy Bible from our young and replaced it with the thoughts of Charles Darwin, Karl Marx, Sigmund Freud and John Dewey."[2] John Dewey was the philosopher mentioned most often in the "secular humanism textbook" trial that took place in Judge Brevard Hand's federal court in Mobile, Alabama, in October, 1986. I was able to attend the first week of the trial and heard many of the plaintiff's expert witnesses mention Dewey. Timothy Smith, a Johns Hopkins historian, said Dewey was an "atheistic humanist"; James Hunter, a University of Virginia sociologist said Dewey was "a Harvard professor"; William Coulson, a California psychologist, declared that Dewey wrote the first Humanist Manifesto and then traced the parentage of values clarification back through its immediate progenitors to Dewey; James Hitchcock, a St. Louis University historian, declared Dewey the "most influential humanist in the twentieth century"; Richard Baer, a Cornell University ethicist, said Dewey was hedonistic. This is, of course, a very distorted view of Dewey that is being offered by the religious right in their attempt to identify John Dewey and humanism as the culprits in the destruction of American education. Some of these assertions are simply contrary to fact. Dewey was never a Harvard professor and, although he signed it, he did not write the Humanist Manifesto. In his correspondence with Corliss Lamont in 1940 he was still willing to stand by the manifesto, but he was insistent that his *philosophy* was best described as a naturalistic rather than a humanistic one.[3] Indeed, it was his natural piety and devotion to shared experience and its values, including justice, community and intelligence, that makes any assertion that he was an atheist or a hedonist problematic.

While it is true that we have gone a long way toward the disestablishment of all forms of Christianity in our public institutions and Dewey played some role in that, it is not the case that a religion of secularism, with Dewey as its chief representative, has been put in Christianity's place. Indeed, the sort of religious secularity proposed by

Dewey in *A Common Faith* is not capable of establishment. It may well be a self-conscious religious practice, but when it ceases to be secular--of this world--and common, it ceases to be acceptable to him as a secular religiosity. Dewey's minimal conditions are that a secular religious practice by firmly situated in this world and a common practice of one's culture. When it becomes either other-worldly or sectarian, it becomes suspect. To think that a sectarian secularism has been established is to regard secularism not only as a religion but to assert that this particular form of secularism is now officially in place in our schools. But the religious right does not make this strong claim. Instead, the claim is that with the disestablishment of Christianity and the pervasiveness of the secular mentality, there has been a de facto establishment of secularism. Even so, the argument will not work without two additional (but problematic) premises: every society is religious and every pervasive belief system is a religion. Then one can argue that if Christianity is no longer our established religion, then something is. This something is a religion of secular humanism.[4]

The religious right's argument depends, to a large extent, on a misunderstanding of "secular" and the Constitutional value of secularity. It takes secular to be "anti-religious"; whereas if fact, although "secular" can sometimes mean this, it can also mean simply "non-religious," having to do with this world and making no references to any other worlds. It is this latter understanding that the Supreme Court had in mind when it formulated the three-prong test that it now uses to determine if there has been an establishment of religion. As stated in Lemon v. Kurtzman (403 US 602, 612-616 [1971], the test reads:

> First, the statute must have a secular legislative purpose; second, its principal or primary effect must be one that neither advances not inhibits religion . . .; finally, the statute must not foster "an excessive government entanglement with religion."

This test rightly assumes there is a large area of our lives which is neither religious nor irreligious. It is not only possible to be non-religious, we are required by the Constitution, as we have seen, to be non-religious, or secular, in our governmental activities.

But there is a conceptual problem. The Constitution, the Bill of Rights and the Supreme Court seem to have little problem with a secular-religious distinction. Our practices can be neatly divided. Those that are secular in intent and effect are permitted governmental activities; those that are religious are not. This distinction, however, depends on an understanding of "secular" as being "non-religious" as opposed to "anti-religious." Originally, the word "secular" meant "of this age" or "this-worldly" and did not deny "the religious" or "the other-worldly." It is this distinction that the Supreme Court used.

This distinction works fairly well if one understands secular and religious to be complementary concepts and government plays a limited role in our lives. This, however, is not perceived to be the case. What has happened (better: culminated) in the twentieth century is that some people have come to see the secular sphere as the only one, thus eliminating the religious one, and government is considered to be omni-present. Thus some conventionally religious people find themselves shut out of the public schools and think some secularists have been permitted to practice their "secular religion" there. The charge in recent court cases in east Tennessee and Mobile, Alabama, is that "secular humanists" use the Supreme Court's neutral understanding of "secular" to practice an anti-traditional "religion of secularism."

If it is the case that constitutionally-required secularity has been corrupted into a religious practice that is suppressing traditional religion, then clearly the judicial system should respond favorably to those who claim that a de facto religious secularism has been established. I do not think, however, that such a religion is the norm in our schools. In order for one to think there is, one must assume that all sorts of practices which many Christians and others do not take to be religious expressions of an anti-traditional religion are in fact a religion of secular humanism. In the court case in east Tennessee, teaching about the Renaissance was alleged to be the replacing of God with a worship of humanity. Or, stories depicting a reversal of traditional sex roles, namely a boy cooking a meal, were cited as denials of Christian teaching. In the Mobile case, textbooks which inform students that "morals are made by people" were claimed to be instances of humanist religion, because humanism, as presented in the Humanist Manifestos espouses a moral relativism. The mind set of these plaintiffs does not seem to recognize the possibility of a Christian humanism that may share certain values with religious humanists, nor, and this is more to the point, recognize that some teaching and belief can be religiously neutral. For the sectarian, there is no non-religious sphere. Recalling, perhaps, the words of Jesus on one occasion, "He who is not with me is against me," the plaintiffs think that every activity is either religious or anti-religious. Thus, that which is not religious in their understanding of "religious" is irreligious, that is, it goes against their particular sectarian stance. Thus, since the values of the Renaissance, feminism and a particular educational strategy that assumes an understanding of the rights of the individual conflicts with their sectarian religion, then it must be anti-religious.

If there is a religion of secularism in the schools, it ought to be rooted out. If not, there is no judicial problem. There is a problem, however, with the sectarian view that everyone in America has an unrestricted right to practice his or her religion without restraint. There is a problem with an understanding of religious freedom that regards the teaching of a point of view that the sectarian finds offensive as a denial of his or her religious freedom. It is to this problem that I now turn.

The Denial of Religious Freedom

No freedom is absolute. We all live within limits. My right of free speech does not permit me to yell "Fire!" in a crowded room. A church's right to practice its religion freely does not permit it to ignore applicable zoning ordinances and fire or health regulations. It must operate its day care center in conformance with all the applicable rules just as any other organization must. To deal with this question, we must pose it in the form in which it arises.

It is the contention of some fundamentalists that their practice of Christianity is being unlawfully restrained by the curriculum of our schools. A curriculum that does not re-enforce or even present views other than the Bible's teachings with regard to man's spirituality or traditional sex roles or the transcendence of God challenges these "Christian" beliefs. Thus a child's faith may be corrupted. If this were to occur, then the parent's right to raise his or her child according to the dictates of his or her faith is being denied. The fundamentalist Christian is at odds at almost every point with a curriculum that is pervasively secular. He or she must then choose between a public education and corruption of the child's faith, on the one hand, and a private education and the free exercise of religion, on the other. To leave the child in school is to forfeit the right to raise the child religiously, as the parent understands her or his religion.

Clearly the notion of secularity as an alternative to religion is still operating here. But what is also present is the belief that one's freedom of religion is absolute. That this cannot be the case can be seen by recalling the original intent of the first amendment religion clauses. It was the recognition that not everyone was of one mind with regard to religion that led the authors of the Bill of Rights to work out a system whereby there would be a private sphere available to sectarians. No one thought there could be unanimity. Conflict, although inevitable, could be limited by restricting it to the non-governmental areas of our lives. There was no presumption that one would be able to practice one's religion in federally-operated institutions. Indeed such was prohibited. Now, with the extension of the Bill of Rights to the states and the provision of public education, we should not presume that one can practice one's religion in the schools. If one's religion conflicts with the common understanding of science, moral education, history and even sex roles, then one can expect a challenge to his or her child's faith in the classroom. The Constitution recognizes my right to hold views peculiar to me; it does not recognize a right for me to demand either that my views be shared by publicly-supported institutions or that my child not be exposed to contrary views.

The Defense of the Common

Although I have argued that a fundamentalist Christian does not have a right to invoke the free exercise clause to prevent his or her child from being exposed to contrary views, I do not want to minimalize the conflict. Clearly, much that is taught in the schools does challenge the views of someone who believes in creationism, the absolute submission of children to parental authority, traditional sex roles and an authoritarian ethic. The schools, many of us would like to think, make use of the best thinking of a variety of disciplines. Oftentimes, this thinking is at variance with traditional views. For instance, in the last interchange in the Mobile trial, a self-described "Christian grandmother" and author of one of the challenged home economics texts defended her non-dogmatic approach. The plaintiffs' lawyer took this very non-dogmatism as evidence of a moral permissiveness that is intolerable to fundamentalist Christians.[5]

For some of the plaintiffs' expert witnesses in the Mobile trial the resolution of this cultural clash is to institute a voucher system. If there can be no neutral position, if all positions are sectarian, then the fair solution is to allow everyone equal access to an education that squares with their sectarian position. This solution is, of course, abhorrent to advocates of public schools. In response the latter often find themselves defending the religious neutrality of the public schools. While this may be a promising defense, it is not necessary to defend objectivism to defend the public schools and their right to teach a secular curriculum. If I am right that the Constitution requires that government institutions should be oriented toward this world, then that is all the justification that defenders of the Constitution need. Of course, one could raise questions about the adequacy of the Constitution as a framework for our nation. But this is not the tack that the religious right takes. They attempt, instead, to use the free exercise clause of the first amendment to argue against secularity. I have responded by saying that if the secularity of the Constitution has degenerated into a sectarian secularism, then indeed their religious freedom is being abridged. But if the secularity of the schools is consistent with the this-worldly secularity of the Constitution, then they do not have a legitimate claim. Rather, they are improperly using one part of the Constitution--the free exercise clause--to argue against the pervasive secularity of the Constitution as a whole.

The real problem that confronts the religious right and others who would give a privileged place to conventional religion is that the Constitution is resolutely secular. Our government is, in spite of session-opening prayers, chaplains in the armed forces and invocations of the deity by presidents--a secular one. It may well be that a largely secular government leaves little room for conventional religion in our society. But this does not constitute an establishment of secularity as a religion. To so argue is to equate secularity and sectarian secularism.

NOTES

1. See Tim LaHaye, *The Battle for the Mind.* (Old Tappan NJ: Fleming H. Revell Company, 1980), pp. 43-45 and 97; Homer Duncan, *Humanism: In the Light of Scripture.* (Lubbock TX: Christian Focus on Government, Inc., 1981), p. 52f. James Hitchcock, *What is Secular Humanism?* (Ann Arbor MI: Servant Books, 1982), p. 12f., and John Whitehead, *The Stealing of America.* (Westchester IL: Crossway Books, 1983), pp. 16-18 and 86f.

2. Dudley Clendinen, "Robertson Sets Conditions for Making a Run in 1988," *The New York Times.* (Thursday, September 18, 1986), p. 16.

3. Lamont, "New Light on Dewey's *Common Faith*," *The Journal of Philosophy* 58 (January 5, 1961).

4. See the second endnote in my "Theology and Agricultural Ethics in the State University: A Reply to Richard Baer," *Agriculture and Human Values* 2 (Fall 1985), 52f., for the many law review articles that argue that there has been a de facto religious establishment of humanism. I have dealt with the religious right's argument in my "Secularity and Religious Establishment," a paper read at the University of Dayton, Fall, 1985.

5. But is this encouragement of a teenager's autonomy evidence of secular humanism? I think not. As one of the defense lawyers pointed out: Just because the Ten Commandments say, "Thou shalt not kill," does not mean that everyone who condemns murder is a Jew or a Christian.

RELIGION, THE CONSTITUTION, AND JOHN DEWEY

A Commentary

E. Paul Colella

Dewey begins his *Human Nature and Conduct* with the proverb, "Give a dog a bad name and hang him. ... Human nature has been the dog of professional moralists . . . ."[1]

Like the dog in the proverb and human nature in moral philosophy, Dewey has been given a bad name by the fundamentalist. Yet the judgment that he deserves the hanging is certainly premature given the distinctions which Professor Eldridge has brought out in his paper. Further evidence seems to suggest that Dewey be spared the criticism which has been directed his way.

It is something of an irony that Dewey is unfairly slandered by his opposition on the religious right when he is blamed for undermining traditional religious ideals, replacing them with more secular and humanistic concerns. Their attack on him is also mistaken in its assessment of the situation and Dewey's role in it. This commentary will develop some issues raised by Professor Eldridge's paper which are relevant to Dewey. First, it is not the inordinate influence of John Dewey but rather the very nature of the modern democratic state which is responsible for the relegation of religion to a private sphere set off against the secular, political world. And second,

Dewey's instrumentalist philosophy is, at its basis, dedicated to the eradication of such artificial dichotomies of which the religious vs. the secular is but an example. What is more, Dewey's thought strives to integrate the religious more fully into the fabric of daily experience. Eldridge is correct in saying that those on the religious right misunderstand the issue which draws so much of their passion. In the case of John Dewey, they target a philosopher whose efforts run in a direction which opposes the absolute schism between the religious and other parts of human experience.

The framers of the Constitution, like so many others involved in modern politics in a theoretical or practical way, owe much to the political ideas of John Locke. This truism is so obvious that it threatens to border on the trivial. The basic methodological premise of Lockean democracy however lies with the distinction between a political sphere of obligation and authority on the one hand, and a pre-political sphere of private rights on the other. Legitimate government, so argues Locke, accepts this division as natural and takes the protection of these pre-political rights of individuals to be the ground of its own proper activity. Similarly, Karl Marx pointed to this division between the political and the private, as well as the decision to locate religion within the private rather than political sphere. As the highest stage of development possible for the modern democratic state itself, it is not an anomaly introduced into it in some artificial way.[2]

But with regard to the fundamentalist's attack against Dewey, there are several issues to be addressed. The first point which needs to be countered is the fundamentalist's assertion that somehow Dewey's philosophical position seeks to divorce religion from political experience. The most casual student of Dewey knows that the creation and maintenance of dualistic dichotomies received sharp and sustained attack from Dewey throughout his career. Such divisions are well-rooted in the Western philosophical tradition, so much so that dualism can be taken to be definitive of that tradition. Nevertheless the persistence of this dualism is an obstacle to the more integrated view of experience as organism-environment interaction which Dewey insists is more "congenial to present conditions."[3] This distinction between a transcendent reality of stable truths, values and ideals superimposed on a spatio-temporal reality of objects and events in process, together with the evaluation of the transcendent as the *genuinely real*, has been attacked by Dewey on so many occasions that to rehearse it again here would be otiose. A practical consequence of such dualism however is that it saps the lifeblood out of values and ideals, including those of the religious variety, their very distance from the lived experience making them irrelevant to the world that they shun. Dewey's criticism of Kant's ethical principles is appropriate here: the ideals become sublime in themselves, but in the end they lack "effective translation into the affairs of the workaday world."[4]

This rejection of dualism as a general element of Dewey's thought is carried over into his consideration of religious matters in *A Common Faith*. "Those who hold to the notion that there is a definite kind of experience which is itself religious" writes Dewey, make it something specific "marked off from experience as aesthetic, scientific, moral, political."[5] The result is a fragmentation of experience into mutually exclusive and independent compartments which in this instance draws "a line between the secular and the profane"[6] and clearly demarcates their respective spheres of influence and concern. In Professor Eldridge's paper, this tendency is most clearly seen in his distinction between the religious and the secular, and in his treatment of "secular" as "anti-religious" and as "non-religious." The unfortunate result is that such bifurcation of religious from secular experience deadens religious ideals which, to many, appear to be foreign to the affairs of daily life and thus are incapable of generating any real loyalty, sometimes even among the religiously committed.

The second point I would like to touch upon follows directly from the foregoing. The fundamentalists are wrong to portray Dewey as the anti-religious secularist. Rather than destroying the religious, Dewey strives to revitalize it as an element in the mainstream of organism-environment interaction. Dewey takes great pains to distinguish *the religious* as an attitude which "can be taken toward every object and every proposed end or ideal" and *a religion* which denotes a special body of beliefs and practices.[7] The distinction, as he notes, is between the adjectival and the substantive. The adjectival interpretation steers clear of introducing the absolute schisms in experience which have come to be associated with the noun and which create a fixed world of "a limited number of classes, kinds, forms, distinct in quality as kinds and species must be distinct."[8] Like the adjective itself, the religious comes to denote a modification of something else, in this case, experience. The religious as Dewey understands it enters into the full flow of experience as an integral component part and is encountered in the most basic features of experience as it is lived.

The active adjustment on the part of the organism to a problematic situation, i.e., the reconstruction of experience itself, possesses its religious dimension. While all religions have insisted upon their ability to "introduce perspective into the piecemeal and shifting episodes of existence," Dewey asserts that it is wrong to attribute this to religion itself. Rather, writes Dewey, "[w]hatever introduces genuine perspective is religious."[9] What is more, the religious and its place in experience must be recognized and extended in the democratic society. Dewey writes that . . .

> Any activity pursued in behalf of an ideal and against obstacles and in spite of threats of personal loss because of conviction of its general and enduring value is religious in quality. Many a person . . . have achieved, without presumption and without display, such unification of themselves and of their relations to the conditions of existence. It remains to extend their spirit and inspiration to ever wider numbers.[10]

Far from being an area of experience which is banished to some isolated sphere, separate and irrelevant to the essential features of experience as Dewey describes these, the religious is ingrained within the very texture of experience itself. The fundamentalist protests this error in his or her own way, but clearly Dewey is not a partisan of those who make such a sharp distinction between the religious and the secular.

In closing, let us note that the fundamentalist is wrong to impose static and non-experimental religious concepts on a fluid and dynamic experience. Similarly, the secularist is wrong to view religion as an irrelevancy which an enlightened humankind has outgrown and has now cast aside. Behind the fundmentalist's quarrel with John Dewey lies the preference for asking one question rather than another. The fundamentalist's perspective chooses to concentrate on the question "what constitutes a religion?" while the more appropriate question to ask according to Dewey's view is "what is the religious dimension of experience?" This preference on the part of fundamentalism, as it turns out, is yet another specimen of the battle between the fixed, closed and compartmentalized universe of the tradition which Dewey rejects and the dynamic, experimental universe of organism-environment interaction that he proposes as its replacement. If this debate teaches us anything, then it must underscore again the inevitable difficulties involved in adopting such a dualism, as well as the peril into which the ideal-producing elements of human life such as religion must fall when they are divorced from the lived experience of real human beings.

NOTES

1. John Dewey, *Human Nature and Conduct*, in *John Dewey: The Middle Works, 1899-1924*, Volume 14: 1922. (Carbondale: Southern Illinois University Press, 1983), p. 4.

2. Karl Marx, "On the Jewish Question," in *Karl Marx: Early Writings*. (New York: Vintage Books, 1975), pp. 216-234.

3. John Dewey, "The Need for a Recovery of Philosophy," in *John Dewey: The Middle Works, 1899-1924*. Volume 10: 1916-1917 (Carbondale: Southern Illinois University Press, 1980), pp. 5-6.

4. John Dewey, "Kant After Two Hundred Years," in *John Dewey: The Middle Years, 1899-1924*. Volume 15: 1923-1924 (Carbondale: Southern Illinois University Press, 1983), p. 11.

5. John Dewey, *A Common Faith*, in *John Dewey: The Later Works, 1925-1953*. Volume 9: 1933-1934 (Carbondale: Southern Illinois University Press, 1986), p. 9.

6. *Ibid*., p. 44.

7. *Ibid*., p. 8.

8. John Dewey, *Reconstruction in Philosophy*, in *John Dewey: The Middle Works, 1899-1924*. Volume 12: 1920 (Carbondale: Southern Illinois University Press, 1982), pp. 110-111.

9. Dewey, *A Common Faith*, in *John Dewey: The Later Works*. Vol. 9: 1933-1934, p. 17.

10. *Ibid*., p. 19.

The author wishes to dedicate this contribution to the memory of his colleague from the Philosophy Department of Xavier University, Professor Alvin C. Marrero.

> "Let us honour thee not so much with transitory praises as with our reverence, and, if our powers permit us, with our emulation."
>
> -Tacitus

THE PROMISE OF POLITICS: HANNAH ARENDT ON THE AMERICAN CONSTITUTIONAL REVOLUTION

William W. Clohesy

We Americans are fortunate in our opportunity to engage in political affairs or to ignore them for the sake of family, business and other private concerns. Our history provides us many examples of political action in realizing common goals such as civil equality which have transpired while allowing some to live strictly private lives. Our experience of politics as both the opportunity for public action and the surety in our own private affairs reflects a balance in the frequently tense relations in modern politics between self-concern and the expansion beyond oneself to a concern for the political community.

Due to its police power, modern politics is often taken to be the legitimate use of force to protect us from another's violence. Locke, for example, defines political power:

> a right of making laws with penalties of death, and consequently all less penalties, for the regulating and preserving of property, of employing the force of the community in the execution of such laws, and the defence of the commonwealth from foreign injury, and all this only for the public good.[1]

More recently Max Weber has commented, "Ultimately, one can define the modern state sociologically only in terms of the *means* peculiar to it, as to every political association, namely, the use of physical force."[2] Modern politics centers upon sovereignty: the rulers hold power over those they rule.

Regardless of the form of government, power over others is the fact of primary importance.

This view of politics could hardly be farther from the classical, for which the opportunity for politics allows one to be excellent on behalf of the city in the presence of others. For the Greeks and Romans, the city made it possible for a citizen to move beyond the private economic affairs of the family to a life in public with others where purposes and values are argued and where deeds are done for the sake of the community, its posterity, and one's own immortality gained in excellent words and deeds. The city permitted the ancients a good life in which citizens devoted themselves to creating a common world of their own design beyond that necessary for survival. Citizens did not act as rulers and ruled in public. They were despots in their homes, from which they gained the leisure to act as citizens. Consequently they were equal to one another and confronted one another only with the force of persuasion. Sovereignty was not an issue. The citizens took turns in office upholding the laws before which they were equal.

While the modern idea of politics as legitimate use of force is widespread, it has not been universally accepted by modern thinkers. Rousseau and Dewey, to name but two, are respectful of the politics of excellence occasionally manifest in modernity. Another philosopher who devoted her life to understanding the perplexities of politics today and sought to reassert excellence as a standard for contemporary politics is Hannah Arendt.

Although she began her studies with an interest in aesthetics, the horror of Europe under the Nazis drew Hannah Arendt inexorably into political philosophy. After the War she settled in the United States, where she wrote extensively and profoundly on political issues. As an American she paid the United States the high compliment of taking the American Revolution seriously and of severely criticizing the failure of American politics. I propose to present here an exposition and interpretation of her understanding that the American Revolution is the most successful of modern political undertakings although in part a failure.

Arendt means more than the War by the term "American Revolution." All revolutions have three moments: the rebellion against a tyranny; the creation of a new form of government which provides for the participation of free citizens; and the establishment of authority, of the respect for those political institutions which now provide that participation. Participation and authority permit a government based upon community, not upon the rule of a sovereign. Community participation, Arendt notes, is the great innovation America offers the modern world. Rebellions which do not end in participative government cannot be called revolutions, for they end where they began, either with the original tyranny still in control or with others in control of the people in turn. Arendt writes, "In this respect, the great and, in the long run, perhaps the greatest American innovation in politics as such was the consistent abolition of sovereignty within the body politic of the republic, the insight that in the realm of human affairs sovereignty and tyranny are the same."[3] If we are to live together politically, we must live as equals for whom persuasion, not coercion, marks our decisions.

Arendt is interested in the American Revolution because it shows the experience, and hence the possibility, of politics based upon participation. Her major study of the Revolution is to be found in *On Revolution*. It has been argued that her treatment taken in itself is poor history: the social upheavals in the States, the confiscation of Tory property, the manipulative dealings to ensure ratification of the Constitution go unmentioned.[4] Her intent, however, is not to write history. Rather, in the story and complex activities of the Revolution, she sees an unmistakable and irreducible occurrence of political freedom. However it might be qualified, the Revolution can teach us many lessons about the structure of political events. Arendt's intent is to bring out the political elements of the Revolution so as to tell a story from which we can gain assurance of our own capacity for political community and for political action.

In an earlier work, *The Human Condition*, Arendt divides human activities into three types: labor, work and action.[5] As are all animals, we are subject to the demands of our metabolism. In order to live we must consume that which we have produced. We labor to maintain a ceaseless cycle of production and consumption. Our labor is ceaseless for, no matter the size of our stores, we will in time exhaust them and need to replenish them. Unlike other animals we can work at fashioning instruments such as tools to ease labor and goods such as houses in which to live in comfort and permanence. Works of art provide our lives with a significance and beauty which are undying. Nonetheless, both labor and work can be done in solitude or isolation. Even an artist working with apprentices can refuse their advice and shun their questions.

Politics does not fit into either of these patterns. For politics cannot be done alone, or through the efforts of others not given a voice in the pattern and purpose of what happens. As members of a political community, we determine among ourselves and *pledge* ourselves to the kind of lives we agree to live. If we praise compassion, for example, we can make it a value manifest in our laws, our education, and our health care. Political actions aim at a future towards which we promise to strive, so that our words and deeds will each resound that promise.

From the ancients we have learned that we humans live as mortals unlike other animals who are immortal in their species. Animals are born, raise their young, and die while their species remains intact. But humans, given the chance to concern themselves beyond hunger and cold, become individuals for themselves in the presence of one another. Their lives are unique for themselves and for others in style and intent.

This is the most fundamental freedom for each human being: the capacity to act beyond the care for bodily needs, the opportunity to take part in the affairs of the community, the chance to make a difference in the world. A human being can develop a personal character and leave traces of individual actions along the way which form the purposive whole of a lifetime. Arendt writes:

> The morality of man lies in the fact that individual lives, a [*bios*] with a recognizable life-story from birth to death rises out of biological life [*zoe*]. This individual life is distinguished from all other things by the rectilinear course of its movement, which so to speak cuts through the circular movements of biological life.[6]

Through our individuality we form a plurality. Arendt explains, "Plurality is the condition of human action because we are all the same, that is, human, in such a way that nobody is ever the same as anyone else who ever lived, lives or will live."[7] Each of us is distinct: our creativity, our conduct and relations with others are our own; they cannot be given by another in our stead. Consequently, our political actions are always each a new initiative or a fresh assertion of the meanings and values to which we devote our lives and which we must leave to others who follow us to continue, to rethink, or to abandon.

Allow me next to review the American Revolution in terms of Arendt's three moments: rebellion, the foundation of freedom, and the establishment of authority.

Rebellion for Independence

Fights for independence are at best the initial step in a revolution. A people with little experience of government and of the complex demands of political freedom, such as respect for opponents, are in danger of falling into a tyranny and of maintaining control through violence against their own people, because these are the forms of rule with which they are familiar.

The people of the fledgling United States could not have been more fortunate. They shared the literature of Shakespeare's plays, so rich in political insight; of Swift's acerbic wit; and of Burke's compelling phrases (as well as his support in Parliament). They had a history of government limited by law and specified civil rights dating back to *Magna Charta* as well as a common law relieving them of the need to begin their judiciary from scratch. They might be separated from Britain through rebellion, but they were separated neither from one another nor from a rich political heritage. Professor Arendt holds

> that the great good fortune of the Americans was that the people of the colonies, prior to their conflict with England, were organized in self-governing bodies, that the revolution--to speak the language of the eighteenth century--did not throw them into a state of nature, that there never was any serious questioning of the *pouvoir constituant* of those who framed the states and, eventually, the Constitution of the United States.[8]

In fact, the *Declaration of Independence* had the immediate effect of inciting the newly free States to the business of constitution-making. Many State constitutions, such as New York's and Virginia's, prefaced their documents with the entire text of the *Declaration*. Yet the Americans were quite careful, indeed conservative, in their handiwork. There were experiments performed such as Pennsylvania's unicameral legislature. For the most part, however, States preserved as much as they could.[9]

The social fabric was not torn as badly in the American Revolution as in the French. The American was a political event; it did not arouse so great an upheaval on questions of property rights, religion and social class. The French Revolution occurred on home territory; more than a political event, it was a class struggle, a religious emancipation, and an economic fight. To say this is in no way to condone or to deny the social inequities in the United States--certainly not slavery. All such problems were expected to have political solutions once political institutions were in place. There was in fact considerable social legislation in the States on problems such as primogeniture and the enlargement of the franchise. It should be noted too that the Southerners at the Federal Convention feared but expected that the Constitution would make slavery and its elimination political issues.

The Constitution

When the War had been won, there were thirteen sovereign States, although there were many ties uniting them. The Articles of Confederation formed a treaty among the States. The citizens of the States could travel freely from one to another. Foreign policy was to be decided in common. Because the Articles were a treaty, the people had no direct voice in it. As well, there was no force in them to compel the States to do what they had agreed to do. The States were moving in different directions economically. The possibility was great that in time they would separate into new groupings of States based upon economic advantage. It was possible that with the War so recently behind them, Americans had only one chance to form an effective union.[10] Sovereignty was the major stumbling block. How could the States organize themselves so that some could not overpower the others?

Whenever power is given to one person or to one committee, no matter how limited by law, it is potentially a means to violence and domination. Arendt describes such power as "the multiplied strength of the one who has monopolized the power of the many."[11] Montesquieu's great discovery, well known to the Founders, is that "it is necessary from the very nature of things that power should be a check to power."[12] We can recognize Montesquieu's insight embodied in the separation of powers by which one branch can deny another the power to act.

While the check to powers is of crucial importance for government, it is the negative side of the basic principle that when people come together and argue toward a consensus for action, they generate the power to act. The separation of powers provides the capacity to halt action. The separation also institutionalizes the unceasing public debate necessary to maintain consensus and the resulting political power. In vetoing a bill, for example, the president returns it "with his objections to that house in which it shall have originated, who shall enter the objections at large in their journal, and proceed to reconsider it." (Article I, section 7) That is, the president opens discussion again toward the formulation of an acceptable bill. The separation of powers is a method for compelling officials to sustain a discourse through which to achieve a thoughtful policy which they can bring others to accept and enact.

A political order rooted in consensus necessarily has a respect for political opinions, for all consensus must be achieved through the interplay, the negation, and the creation of opinions which allow the group to reach decisions for the public good. James Madison argues, "When men exercise their reason coolly and freely on a variety of distinct questions, they inevitably fall into different opinions on some of them. When they are governed by a common passion, their opinions, if they be so called, will be the same."[13] Individuals, possessing different experiences, needs and hopes, will naturally disagree on many issues. Self-interest and disagreement in small communities can lead to rancor and resentment. People moved by passion from--or are rendered by demogogues--factious mobs.

Madison sees a protection from faction in the great size of the United States. Direct democracy, subject to popular passions, is unworkable in any country, but impossible in so large a country. If the people want self-rule, a representative government alone can work. There is less danger of paralyzing factions among a select group of peers from places having quite different interests. These representatives (by which I mean all elected officials and those appointed by them) coming to the capital will find others from all over the country. For representatives to be effective they cannot simply repeat the interests of those back home. They need to deliberate toward a shared image of the country's interests, even if these interests do not fully correspond with those of their constituents. Through this process Madison hopes that representatives, gaining insights through working with others in public office, will develop an enlarged perspective on the whole republic. The resulting decisions should far better suit the country than decisions taken solely for some particular interest by representatives heedless or ignorant of more encompassing needs of the nation.

Representatives, for their own re-election, must take their insights home and, through explaining their work on the community's behalf, raise the level of awareness of political affairs among the public. A system of discourse should take place both horizontally among those in government and vertically between representatives and the electorate. The several States comprise yet another group of participants in this discussion. A republican form of government exists within every State. And the States themselves have positions which they can present as corporate persons to the national government. The goal of this complex process of discourse is that laws and policy will express the enlarged common interest, which would be as impossible to divine at the local level alone as it would be at the national level by officials cut off from intercourse with the people themselves.

Madison's achievement is to shift the focus off claims of sovereignty and to place it upon an *activity* most familiar to Americans: political debate and the search for consensus. His emphasis is on an action, not an office. Who is the American sovereign? Congress has primacy because it makes the laws. Yet it can be checked. Can one say that the president represents the American people in some way better than Congress assembled? He might wish to; but under criticism for controversial proposals, the primacy of Congress is quickly reasserted. To speak of an American sovereign is, properly, to speak of the Constitution at work.

Although it has been charged time and again that the Constitutional system was designed to remove power from the people's hands, the people are crucial for this system to work. They must elect shrewd, far-seeing, and articulate men and women to office. All rests finally on the people who elect those through whom the general good is to be decided. Only so long as the people retain a republican character and seriously study public affairs and press their representatives on them will the republican system of government work. As well, the institutions of government need the respect of the people. Leaders need trust in their decisions and laws, for doubt and cynicism turns a populace litigious and resentful of all change and sacrifice.

Authority

The Constitution provides institutions which make possible political action. As are all political actions, the Constitution is a beginning aimed at a future. The Founders began a tradition in which the republic is turned over to successive generations to maintain and improve. With its foundation and tradition comes the Constitution's authority. The institutions for political action are treated with awe: so much of our world follows from the agreements and precedents stretching back to the beginning. All who follow in the tradition of these institutions have a duty to uphold it. Our duty does not flow from the use of force or power, but from our reverence for the institutions. When one must be persuaded or coerced to respect an authority, it is no longer an authority. For Americans the Founders' Constitution stands as an authority unifying our political history as it unfolds from the originary act of beginning itself.[14]

Something is amiss. The only fitting veneration for the creation of institutions for political action is continued political action. The failure of the Constitution, Arendt holds, is its failure to provide for sustained political action by the citizenry as a whole. The Constitution provides for action at the State and national level, but it ignores the local politics of townships, wards and precincts. The people were only given the task of electing representatives; the "Constitution had given all power to the citizens, without giving them the opportunity of being republicans and of *acting* as citizens."[15] Voting alone offers meager and sporadic political action.

The opportunity to act on public matters has come to be monopolized by office-holders and -seekers and the functionaries of the political parties. The result is that people are forced back into private affairs, from which perspective public matters can be seen only in the light of one's own interests. People who do not study and rigorously argue about public questions cannot develop the enlarged opinions necessary for dispassionate decisions.[16] So far as parties use marketing techniques and have a monopoly on who the candidates are, "they are . . . the very efficient instruments through which the power of the people is curtailed and controlled."[17] Political activity is fast becoming a business in which representatives have careers, political staffs hold jobs, and the policies pursued are formulated by experts with a skilled eye upon popular opinion. Arendt concludes that "what we today call democracy is a form of government where the few rule, at least supposedly, in the interest of the many. This government is democratic in that popular welfare and private happiness are its chief goals; but it can be called oligarchic in the sense that public happiness and public freedom have again become the privilege of the few."[18] Government is increasingly a private matter, concerned with the personal welfare of its participants and beneficiaries.

There are no provisions for local political action in the Constitution; that does not mean, however, that political action by individuals is impossible. Political action is a basic human capacity, although it does not develop instinctively. We must learn it with others and through the stories of political deeds. Thus, the Founders have given us a heritage that will remain ours as long as we remember their *deeds* and not only their words. In America political action arises among people in turmoil, be they women's groups, block associations or school committees, often with no affiliation to political parties or government offices. Such political events indicate that there are some who want a say in the course of their country. People need a voice in the direction of their own communities if they are to become skilled in political action. They need, moreover, a series of associations providing continuity and communication from the local to the national level of politics and back. Although overshadowed by "official" political display, political actions still shine out here and there in America.[19] Hannah Arendt's point is that we *can* act politically.

I began by mentioning that we Americans are free to participate in politics or not, as we wish. Arendt's thought indicates a strange inversion in American public life: private affairs are the concern of much of government today, but public affairs are the concern of active citizens all around us. Now, more than ever before, mindful of the power generated through political action, we should recognize that politics and government are not the same thing.

NOTES

1. John Locke, *An Essay Concerning the True Original, Extent and End of Civil Government (The Second Treatise)* in *The English Philosophers from Bacon to Mill.* (New York: The Modern Library, 1939), paragraph 3, p. 404.

2. Max Weber, "Politics as a Vocation," in *From Max Weber; Essays in Sociology*, trans., ed., with an Introduction by H. H. Gerth and C. Wright Mills. (New York: Oxford University Press, 1946), pp. 77-78.

3. Hannah Arendt, *On Revolution.* (New York: The Viking Press, 1963), p. 152.

4. See Robert Nisbet, "Hannah Arendt and the American Revolution," *Social Research* 44 (Spring, 1977) 63-79; James Miller, "The Pathos of Novelty: Hannah Arendt's Image of Freedom in the Modern World," in Melvin A. Hill, ed., *Hannah Arendt: The Recovery of the Public World.* (St. Martin's Press, 1979), pp. 177-208.

5. Hannah Arendt, *The Human Condition.* (Chicago: The University of Chicago Press, 1958).

6. Hannah Arendt, *Between Past and Future*, enlarged ed. (New York: The Viking Press, 1968), p. 42.

7. Arendt, *The Human Condition*, p. 8.

8. Arendt, *On Revolution*, p. 164.

9. The following, in the Constitution of the State of New York of 1777, is typical of the period: "AND BE IT FURTHER ORDAINED, That all grants of land within this state, made by the king of Great Britain, or persons acting on his authority after the fourteenth day, one thousand seven hundred and seventy-five, shall be null and void. But that nothing in this constitution contained shall be construed to affect any grants of land within this state, made by the authority of said king or his predecessors. . .prior to that day."

10. An account of the troubles facing the country can be found in James Madison's "Preface" to his *Notes of Debates in the Federal Convention*, ed., with an Introduction by Adrienne Koch (Athens, Ohio; Chicago; London: Ohio University Press, 1984).

11. Arendt, *On Revolution*, p. 150.

12. Charles Secondat, Baron de Montesquieu, *The Spirit of the Laws*, trans. Thomas Nugent, with an Introduction by Franz Neumann. (New York: Hafner Press, 1949), Book XI, chapter 4, p. 151.

13. Federalist No. 50 in Alexander Hamilton, John Jay and James Madison, *The Federalist Papers*, with an Introduction, Table of Contents, and Index of Ideas by Clinton Rossiter. (New York and Scarborough: New American Library, 1961), p.319.

14. See Arendt, *On Revolution*, pp. 200-205. Also see her essay, "What is Authority?" in *Between Past and Future*.

15. Arendt, *On Revolution*, p. 256.

16. *Ibid*., p. 272.

17. *Ibid*., p. 273.

18. *Ibid*.

19. See *Ibid*., pp. 282f; and Hannah Arendt, "Thoughts on Politics and Revolution" and *Crises of the Republic*. (New York: Harcourt Brace Jovanovich, A Harvest Book, 1972), pp. 230ff.

THE PROMISE OF POLITICS

A Commentary

Mary L. Sabato

In his "exposition," Mr. Clohesy has given a fairly general description of a very rich, coherent body of Arendt's thoughts on the American Revolution.[1] In order to be able to evaluate her conclusions regarding the Revolution's achievement or its failure, we need to know (1) her specific criteria for a successful revolution, and (2) why she chose precisely those criteria.

Arendt has only two requisites for a successful revolution. The first is that the men of the revolution should found a new body politic. That means framing a constitution which will create a space for freedom. Freedom, to her, means nothing more nor less than political action, because politics is the action of man par excellence. ". . . for action and politics . . . are the only things of which we could not even conceive without at least assuming that freedom exists . . ."[2] Thus comes the necessity for freedom's place in the body politic. Only public action, that convening of persons in open forum to determine their collective fate, is political action proper. Only this action, in its uncoerced spontaneity and novelty, always has the possibility in it of a new beginning. Furthermore, Arendt believes, politics, and nothing else, precipitates that sense of well-being or well-living called "public happiness."

Arendt's second criterion for a successful revolution is then, logically enough, to ensure the continuance of public happiness. That is done by ensuring that every man has a space to be seen and heard and to see and hear others. This, to her, is the Spirit of Revolution itself.[3]

Arendt notes that prior to the 18th Century, "revolution" was a term used to describe the usurpation of one ruler by another. A head of state was supplanted by his ouster and the *form* of government remained intact. In the 18th Century French and American Revolutions, however, the bodies politic themselves were ousted and constitutions were written to establish the bodies of entirely new governments. Here we have an evolution of revolution. No longer does "revolution" mean to revolve back to the beginning, but means to become itself a beginning. "Beginning"/"natality" is, for Arendt, characteristic of revolution. Yet, she believes, only the space for freedom is provided by a constitution. Freedom exists in fact only so long as people engage one another in the political arena. Only in public debate and collective decision making does the Spirit of freedom flourish, for only here is there always the possibility of a new beginning.

If, as Arendt has charged, the Framers of our Constitution made no explicit provision for direct participation in government at the local level of politics, this omission should not be construed as oversight. Arendt herself maintains that public happiness was manifest in the political lives of the men of the American Revolution even before the war itself. Citizens were used to convening in order to deliberate about their common problems in meeting halls and public squares throughout the American colonies. This was all a matter of course. She claims that the Revolution occurred in fact before the Revolutionary War was fought. Nevertheless, she argues that the Founders forfeited the citizens' right to direct participation in government at the local levels by not explicitly incorporating provisions for that right into the body politic.

The Founders understood, I contend, that public happiness is most alive when citizens can achieve the end of revolution for themselves. Establishing one's own government in which one determines how and that one shall participate in public affairs, was left to the people themselves to accomplish. How should we experience public happiness if it is pre-ordained that we shall do so? No free act can be pre-determined. One cannot be commanded to be free. The First Amendment does not say, "The people *shall* peaceably assemble." The Framers of our Constitution did not legislate freedom because they could not. No one can. We can only create a space for it--allow for it. In this vein, Amendment X reserves for the people all rights not expressly prohibited by law. This, I maintain, is the Founders' recognition of citizens' rights too numerous to mention or to even be knowable to them. Our forefathers understood that they could never anticipate the specific requirements of citizens of all places and times.

This *carte blanche*, as it were, ironically provides the opportunity, via the law, to relinquish or to suppress political action, as well as to engage in it. A glaring case in point is the Smith Act of 1940, 18 *U.S.C.S.* Sec. 2385. The Smith Act revokes the right of every citizen to revolution. It makes liable for substantial fine or imprisonment

> Whoever knowingly or wilfully advocates, abets, advises, or teaches, the duty, necessity, desirability, or propriety of overthrowing or destroying the government of the United States . . .[4]

This directly contradicts the Declaration of 1776, which states:

> But when a long train of abuses and usurpations, pursuing invariably the same object evinces a sign to reduce them [mankind, i.e.] under absolute Despotism, it is their right, it *is* their duty, to throw off such Government, and to provide new guards for their future security. [my emphasis][5]

John Somerville reports ("The Contemporary Significance of the Declaration of Independence"):

> When I appeared in a Smith Act trial in Philadelphia as an expert witness on revolutionary doctrines, I was actually forbidden by the judge to mention the Declaration of Independence.[6]

When such a law is upheld in the courts and citizens conform to its writ, the space for freedom shrinks drastically. So long as such statutes are not revoked from the body politic, they may be invoked by the executors of government. So long as they are invoked, they revoke the foundations of freedom in the body politic. Then, unless the citizens renounce that invocation in word and deed, the Spirit of Revolution is a phantom and public freedom is extinguished.

Ultimately, the Spirit of Revolution is secured in public acts of freedom. No written corpus can provide what it is in the nature of the spirit to do. Arendt has said, "Men are free . . . as long as they act, neither before nor after . . ."[7] If she could listen closely to her own words, she would find the insurance of freedom to be as short-lived as its reality. Would that she could recall her own observation that the Revolution in America had occurred before the writing of the Constitution; that the inspiration for revolution precedes its incorporation, not vice versa. Then she must know that the pact through which we pledge "our lives, our fortunes, and our sacred honor" can only be a reminder, not a provider of freedom.

If the Spirit of Revolution wanes, it is not because, as Clohesy says, "The opportunity to act on public affairs has come to be monopolized" by anyone; it is not because, as he says, "People are forced back to private affairs." It is not, as Arendt says, because "the power of the people is curtailed and controlled" by party machines.[8] It is not because of anything that can be expressed in the passive voice. It is because of what can only be expressed truthfully in the active voice. Public happiness declines when people relinquish their power to the party; when people acquiesce to political charlatans; when people abandon the space preserved for them by those who do not relinquish, acquiesce, and abandon.

Grass roots political freedom existed prior to the Constitution of 1787. That Constitution does not explicitly revoke that freedom. It does implicitly guarantee it for whomever would have it. Then, I submit, if we would implicate some culprit who jeopardizes the Spirit of Revolution, who deteriorates the fabric of freedom, we must look not to the Constitution, but to its constituents.

NOTES

1. William W. Clohesy, "The Promise of Politics: Hannah Arendt on the American Constitutional Revolution."

2. Hannah Arendt, *Between Past and Future* (Harmondsworth, Middlesex, England: Penguin Books Ltd., 1968), p. 146.

3. Hannah Arendt, *On Revolution* (Harmondsworth, Middlesex, England: Penguin Books Ltd., 1965), pp. 125-7.

4. *Smith Act, U.S. Code*, vol. 18, Sec. 2385 (1940).

5. John Somerville, "The Contemporary Significance of the American Declaration of Independence," *Philosophy and Phenomenological Research* 38 (June 1978)489.

6. *Ibid.*, p. 497.

7. Arendt, *Past and Future*, p. 153.

8. Clohesy.

AN AESTHETIC GLANCE AT THE CONSTITUTION: STYLE, INTENTION, PERFORMANCE[1]

Morris Grossman

That language has different functions is one of philosophy's recurrent claims--if not one of its actual insights. These functions have been explained with the help of different typologies--sometimes using simple terms like "informative," "directive," and "expressive"; sometimes with subtler (though comparable) terms like "assertive," "active," and "exhibitive." Several functions of language can obtain simultaneously, e.g., the aesthetic (expressive, exhibitive) and the moral (directive, active)--though one is usually thought to prevail. "Thou shalt not kill" has its touch of eloquence, as does the Golden Rule. But such statements are essentially moral precepts, laws, rules or commandments. What artistry they have is secondary. To dwell on the artistry, when something else is more important, might seem a misguided, if not a perverse, aestheticism. Surely the Constitution is primarily a legal or moral document, not an aesthetic one.[1] In terms of the aforementioned distinctions, it is informative and directive, not exhibitive.

However, the Constitution is not without art. Looking at it aesthetically--creatively misreading it, taking the text for something other than it obviously is--can be a way of gaining unexpected insights.[2] Even deliberate distortion, as in caricature, underlines as it undermines the truth of what was distorted. Hermeneutics at its best surely involves an openness to the mysteries and obscurities of texts, their multiplicities of function, and the possibility of various critical approaches. Here I make some remarks about the Constitution from an aesthetic perspective. While I use three headings--style, intention and performance--they are actually interrelated and inseparable. And I single out Gouverneur Morris for his important but neglected role in creating the Constitution.

Style

The Founding Fathers were themselves not without an interest in literary artistry. They were habitual and practiced readers and writers. Their concern about style as such is a tribute to their awareness of the connections between linguistic form and substance. Proposals and drafts at the Constitutional Convention were referred, in the final days, to the Committee on Style. The five members of the committee were from Harvard, Yale, Princeton, with two from Columbia.

Fashioning a good text is rarely a joint enterprise, and ungainly camels, we know, are created by committees. Elegance and shapeliness require an individual hand. Gouverneur Morris, though not the chair of the Committee on Style, was the decisive fashioner of the document and it was he who gave the Constitution its literary cast. Overall, he was second only to James Madison in his textual and other contributions, and spoke up during the Convention even more than Madison did. Taking style and substance together, looking at the Constitution in its broadest scope, Morris can be said to have been its author.

Gouverneur Morris was an outstanding writer, eventually about matters as varied as fiscal policy and the French Revolution. An elitist and aristocrat, cultivated and witty, he had read widely in Shakespeare, Sterne and Swift. Morris had his own constitutional agenda--a powerful president elected for life, a Senate appointed by the President, suffrage to property holders, etc. But these preferences were essentially aesthetic and detached, and not connected with political and financial ambitions--of which (compared with so many of the other Founders) he was relatively free. As the dramatic orchestrator of the Constitution, as someone always ready to relinquish his personal preference for a gained harmony, Morris's human and intellectual traits were precisely the ones that were needed for the task. Those mincing critics of Morris, who praised his brilliance but mistrusted him and despoiled his character, simply did not understand the source and scope of his contribution.

The Constitution was hammered together out of enormously competing interests. Gouverneur Morris, and his Committee on Style, did more than superficially modify the texts that were handed over. As aestheticians remind us, poetry is not spread on prose the way butter is spread on bread, and style is not a gloss on substance. Style in a measure is substance. The force of the Constitution is not only in its precise and prosaic details ("The president shall serve . . .") but in its occasional moral eloquence, its well chosen and provocative phrases, and not least of all, its cultivated ambiguities. The artistry and the eloquence of the document have influenced how it has been honored, and hence have been factors in its practical effectiveness as an enduring instrument. The ambiguities have invited, indeed necessitated, interpretation.[3]

To be sure, creating language that was occasionally cryptic and vague (Morris was particularly good at this) had the immediate practical function of making acceptable to the Convention what otherwise would not have been accepted. But it also left leeway for future interpretations which specificity would have constrained. Whatever the reasons for the vaguenesses, and the "intentions" behind them, the possibility of varied interpretation is inherent in the document, and is one of its most important stylistic properties.

The gift of vagueness, stylistically understood, is not an aberration of the power of precision, nor is it even distinct from it. Morris's capacity for vagueness went hand in hand with his skill at streamlining language, and giving it strength, grace and economy. When necessary, he could and did eliminate downright sloppiness of construction. Morris was the Convention's English professor as well as its literary artist, and shifted easily between his creative and remedial roles.

Item. Consider Article I, section 8, clause 10. At one point the Committee on Style had this before it. "To define and punish piracies and felonies committed on the high seas, and punish offences against the law of nations." Morris removed the second "punish" so that "define and punish" would carry over from the previous clause, an apparent instance where precision and streamlining went together.[4]

But even here there was a subtler relationship between precision and vagueness than meets the eye. To the objection (from James Wilson) that it would be arrogant of one nation to pretend to define the law of nations, Morris objected that the latter was often too vague and deficient to be enforceable without statutory definition! Morris could create or undo vagueness with equal skill. To summarize the point, when vagueness is not mere confusion it is grounded in precision and, as in Romantic art, is a calculated departure from it.

The transformation of substance by style is best seen in the preamble. The original draft went as follows:

> We the people of the States of New Hampshire, Massachusetts, Rhode-Island and Providence Plantations, Connecticutt, New-York, New-Jersey, Pennsylvania, Delaware, Maryland, Virginia, North-Carolina, South-Carolina, and Georgia do ordain, declare, and establish the following constitution for the Government of Ourselves and our Posterity.

Omitting the states in the actual preamble made the document more open textured, inviting the states that would actually sign to a performative action that determined the initial scope of the union. The preamble also veered the emphasis from the states to the people, and added the vagueness of the phrases "establish justice," "insure domestic tranquility, "promote the general welfare" and "blessings of liberty." Some have argued that the Preamble is not itself a substantive part of the Constitution, that it states purposes, but assigns no powers. But they have simply neglected the actual power of artistic eloquence and stylistic embellishment, its important invitation to interpretation, and its practical consequences.

Intention

Intention and intentionality are variously explored and puzzled over in life, law, psychology, ethics and aesthetics. Ever since the Beardsley-Wimsatt essay, aestheticians have had at intention with a vengeance.[5] My guiding assumption here is that aestheticians have seen sooner than others, and more clearly, the pitfalls associated with attributions of intention. Specifically, the lesson of the "intentional fallacy" is that the artist's intentions are perhaps interesting, but do not have much bearing upon, let alone exhaust, the meaning and value of an artwork. Artists are not privileged with respect to knowing their intentions, and even their precisely stated intentions do not reflect what they have accomplished. The wider value, then, of looking at the "intentional fallacy," with its undermining of naivetes and assurances about artworks, has been to raise comparable questions about any intentions--not only the artist's. Just as it is risky to attribute a clear and univocal intention to an artist, it is equally precarious to do so with a law giver or a legal document. Such attribution is a political or moral act of interpretation, itself in need of further interpretation. The dogma of univocal intention is an interpretation which tries to close off further study and interpretation. The "intentional fallacy" then, though originated in discussions of art, is remarkably relevant to all kinds of persons and documents, not least of all to the Constitution. I offer one example of the absurdity of laying too great store by "the intention of the Founding Fathers," and of how we can commit the "intentional fallacy" with respect to the Constitution. I quote from *Mr Madison's Constitution* by Frank Donovan.

> The Committee of Detail had reported that new states should "be admitted on the same terms with the original states." This displeased most of the delegates, particularly Gouverneur Morris, who claimed that he "did not mean to discourage the growth of the western country. . . . He did not wish, however, to throw the power into their hands." The Convention readily agreed to his substitution: "New states may be admitted by the legislature into the Union." This clause was so ambiguous that it could be interpreted in any of a variety of ways. Sixteen years later, in reply to an inquiry about the Louisiana Purchase, Morris himself interpreted it by writing: "Your inquiry . . . is substantially whether the Constitution can admit, as a new state, territory which did not belong to the United States when the Constitution was made. In my opinion, they cannot. I have always thought that, when we should acquire Canada and Louisiana, it would be proper to govern them as provinces, and allow them no voice in our councils." Had Morris had his way, Florida, Texas, California, Alaska, Hawaii, and several other states would now be provinces."[6]

So much for the intention of one Founding Father with respect to his own Constitutional text! The wonder is that Gouverneur Morris was a Founding Father, and not a Loyalist. Sticking with George III would have been natural to his temperament, consistent with some of his in-laws, and much in accord with what I would call--with obvious glibness and irony--his deepest "intention."

Performance

Interpretation is closely connected with both style and performance. Symphonies and plays are performed, and aestheticians have wondered about the moral and aesthetic mysteries attendant upon acting in a drama or playing a piano sonata. There is an obligation to an original, a text or score, but also an obligation, in performing it, to interpret creatively, to do something which in the nature of the case cannot be rule-governed and precise. Aestheticians have been aware of, have carefully spelled out, the ambiguity of these separate obligations. They exist together; they tug against each other; each needs to be honored, and there is no finality in any one performance decision with respect to how they are separately honored.

As with a literary text or musical score, so with the Constitution. "Playing it" needs to be seen in its double aspects, as an occasion for and indeed as requiring both freedom and constraint.[7] Performance demands not only fidelity to the text or score (as legalists would like it), but meta-attention, so to speak, to the array of options between what is prescribed, and what is left unprescribed.

The Constitution is a text, a score, which has much in it, admittedly, that is clearly and narrowly prescriptive. Its details have at times been ignored, or performed not badly but wrongly, even by those who have dutifully sworn to uphold it. It is possible to show how, where and when this has happened. But as a text, it is open to interpretation and invites interpretation. Respect for it, like respect for a work of art, is not realized by attending only to its precisions and its demands and by refusing to interpret; it is manifested by attending to its possibilities and daring to interpret. Interpretation and performance go hand in hand. Interpretation might be said to be the words that explain the original text. Performance might be said to be the executive, legislative and judicial decisions, depending upon interpretation, that have accumulated in the making of the tradition.

Because the Constitution prescribes a great deal in unequivocal detail, it is sometimes mistakenly (unaesthetically!) seen as imperfect for failing to prescribe everything; or it is mistakenly seen as capable of prescribing everything--if one could discover the original intentions of its authors. Composers sometimes specify *a piacere*, in a precisely articulated invitation to freedom. Any critical study of the Constitution, and of its history, shows that it implies such invitations.

We are keenly aware of the freedoms we enjoy, or think we enjoy, because concretely specified in so many words in the Bill of Rights. We are perhaps not as readily aware of the importance of the open texture and built in drama of the Constitution. Judge Antonin Scalia made this point effectively in the hearings before the Senate Judiciary Committee.

> The nominee said the Bill of Rights, which includes freedom of speech and the right to a trial by an impartial jury, would be meaningless if it were not for the rest of the Constitution. "If you put your finger on what makes our Constitution so enduring," he said, "I think it's the original document before the amendments were added, because the amendments themselves don't do anything. ... The Russian Constitution probably has better or at least as good guarantees of personal freedom as our Constitution does," he said. "What makes it work, what assures that those words are not just hollow promises, is the structure of government that the original Constitution established, the checks and balances among the three branches of government so no one of them is able to run roughshod over the liberties of the people.[8]

No one of the branches is able to ride roughshod over the others because the three are part of a dramatic (i.e., artistic) structure, and not a logical one. The relation between the branches, since it is not precisely and logically given, needs to be constantly determined and invented by active interpretation and performance.

In those instances in the Constitution where there is some attempt to specify checks and balances, we have possible inconsistency or paradox, and some loss of needed open texture. For example, Article III, Section 2, "In all the other cases before mentioned the Supreme Court shall have appellate jurisdiction, both as to law and fact, with such exception, and under such regulations as the Congress shall make." Such "exceptions" and "regulations" could run head on against the Supreme Court's power of judicial review, intimated by Article VI, Section 2, and Article III, Section 1.

Contradictions in a legal text tend to be looked upon as mistakes while contradictions in a literary text (e. g., Plato) are (or can be) seen as part of a dramatic structure. Here we do well to see that even a legal text, or what is essentially a legal text, can be buttressed by non-logical components. Going even further, and keeping the Russian Constitution in mind, we might say that a legal text can be too tightly structured.[9] In a word, the resilient richness of the artistry of the Constitution is neither a gloss, nor legally irrelevant; it is the whole thing, and it influences how it has worked. The ultimate artistry of the document lies beyond all overt specificity and all covert intention, certainly beyond any one interpretation or performance.

At the birth of the Constitution, and for some time thereafter, there were grave doubts about its merits. Hamilton could call it "worthless." John McHenry gave as a reason for having signed the Constitution that he distrusted his own judgment! Gouverneur Morris himself was thoroughly disillusioned with it a quarter of century after fashioning it. In 1815, he was ready to have New York and New England secede from the union!

Though we are now in the midst of honoring the Constitution, there are lots of differing opinions about both its weaknesses and its merits. However, even some of those who see the Constitution as flawed recognize its "mythic" might, its positive power (which must be essentially inspirational and aesthetic) to offset the deficiencies of its details. The ongoing reevaluations of the Constitution are reminiscent (to pursue my analogy) of the way works of art require time and testing and performance to manifest their richnesses, and of the way in which historical judgments keep changing. The matter is never finally settled.

George Washington sent the new Constitution to Congress, with a covering letter drafted (characteristically!) by Gouverneur Morris. It said, "it is not easy to be wise for all times, not even for the present, much less for the future . . . ." I, for one, hope that the Constitution will continue to be performed in a hundred years, at its tricentennary celebration.[10] If we think to know now how it will then be interpreted, we are artless in our vision of history.

NOTES

1. Some years ago (April 4, 1975), I organized a Symposium at Fairfield University on Art and Law. I draw ideas from it.

2. Aesthetic approaches in these areas are not unusual. For example, *The Authority of Publius*, by Albert Furtwangler (Cornell University Press), applies literary and stylistic considerations to the Federalist papers. The Declaration of Independence has been studied stylistically in great detail.

3. Cf. *Cracks in the Constitution*, by Ferdinand Lundberg (Secaucus NJ: Lyle Stuart Inc., 1980), p. 128.

4. Edward Dumbauld, *The Constitution of the United States* (University of Oklahoma Press, 1964), pp. 160, 161.

5. William K. Wimsatt and Monroe C. Beardsley, "The Intentional Fallacy," reprinted in *Problems in Aesthetics*, ed. Morris Weitz (1970).

6. Frank Donovan, *Mr. Madison's Constitution* (New York: Dodd, Mead and Co., 1965), pp. 69, 70.

7. Ibid. "For the power to interpret is the power to introduce trills, cadenzas and thematic variations, giving us what is metaphorically called 'The Living Constitution,' " p. 33.

8. *The New York Times*, August 6, 1986.

9. Faculty who have ever worked on Handbooks and Grievance Procedure documents have sometimes discovered that loose structure leaves free what wordiness binds.

10. I would no more want radical restagings of the Constitution than I would of Mozart's "Don Giovanni," which was fashioned concurrently with the Constitution in 1787.

THE AESTHETICS OF THE CONSTITUTION: COMMENTARY ON MORRIS GROSSMAN

Robert Ginsberg

How refreshing to examine the Constitution aesthetically! We are grateful to Morris Grossman for this graceful opening of such considerations, focusing on style, intention, and performance or interpretation.

Style is not limited to finding the most strategic word for a point, though often the Constitution's strategy is to use the general or ambiguous word, as Morris Grossman points out. An eighteenth-century model of style as enlightened discourse permeates this public document's famous preamble. The Constitution opens with an elevated voice, as befits its solemn and momentous occasion. It speaks out across the ages. Its noble tone is not the style of an individual or group. Instead, this is the high verbal act of a people. The endowment of a people with the noble style is thrilling. Something new in the human order announces itself with those words, "We the People."

The preamble, only a sentence, is one of the Enlightenment's most eloquent public utterances. Its noble vision, stirring cadence, and grand commitment are compelling. The Constitution should not be viewed as the dry setting down of legal rules and political restrictions. It is an attempt to show forth the good in the arrangement of human life such that its truth is evident. There is an aesthetic resonance to this kind of high recognition.

Aestheticians, Morris Grossman reminds us, have largely overcome the temptation to read into works of art statements of their artists, and we should avoid the fallacy when dealing with the Constitution. But legal scholarship does admit, for better or worse, tracing the intentions of the framers of legislation. This legislative context, usually found in the Congressional debates and hearings, is but one resource of interpretation, along with precedence, reasoning, and other considerations. Yet the Constitution was meant to be immune from such questioning of the motives of its framers, as their proceedings were not to be published. We cannot even count upon the *Federalist Papers*, which were privately and anonymously written arguments sent to newspapers. The Constitution, then, comes to us severed from the intentions of those who had a hand in it, and it thereby bears its own intentions.

The Constitution is a discourse vibrant with intentionality. It is a purposive composition. The preamble sets forth the noblest goals conceivable for a people and then enacts the Constitution for those purposes. While the specific purposes may be mentioned again only occasionally in the Constitution, they are the guiding presence of the whole text. They also make the Bill of Rights right at home as directly addressing such purposes. The Constitution is a normative discourse, committed to values, aiming at goals, and selecting what will serve best.

Another aesthetic dimension of the Constitution is personification. This applies not as the figure of speech, for probably no figures of speech appear in the text, but as a sense of narrative presence, a persona. We the people are the self-announced persona and the Constitution might be thought of as the adventures of the people in establishing a new world for their fulfillment. The noble tone and the normative pursuit are related in this towering persona, this new Leviathan. The people create the Constitution. Although Article 7 provides for ratification by the states, that is a final instrumentality, for at the outset the people "ordain and establish" the Constitution for the country. That the people are the creator of the work is all the more reason not to refer to the intentions of the framers, who must have been mere agents of the creator.

The Constitution as a created edifice is mostly new. Article 4 on the states is the principal reference to what is existent. Otherwise the edifice is not an adaptation of what is in place. Whatever real political structures or powers were at play in the twelve years since the independence of the United States (signalled in the dating by the Constitutional Convention), the Constitution speaks the language of innovation. It is not descriptive, and its prescriptions are initiatory. The Constitution, in other words, is an invention. To press the aesthetic connection: the Constitution is the art by which a people assures its destiny. And that art takes on the appearance of genius because of its independence in creation, its clarity of form and statement, its elevation of style, and its heroic presence of creator.

The hero of the piece is the people who raise the curtain with their presence. The first Article deals with that form of the government which is closest to the people: the legislative. But the people do not legislate. Their legislative power is transformed into two houses of Congress (Section 1). That house which is chosen by the people is mentioned first (Section 2). But here the Constitution must at length go into who the people are and how they are to be counted for the sake of electing the popular house. In contrast to the Representatives who speak for every corner of the nation during terms of two years, the Senators serve six years and are not chosen by the people but by the legislatures of each state. The popular house is responsible for originating all revenue bills (Section 7). When the powers of Congress are spelled out in Section 8 we hear echoes of the preamble ("provide for the common defence and general welfare") such that of all of the powers in the edifice, the legislative in Article 1 appears most directly concerned with the goals of its creator, the people. Articles 2 and 3 on the executive and judicial dimensions then appear as prudent modifications of the power of the legislative.

Morris Grossman suggests the aesthetic analogy of a musical score that is given varied though legitimate interpretation over the years in performance. I suggest architecture as model for appreciation of the Constitution. The composition erects a three-winged structure whose center is the legislative. Protected walkways connect each wing, just as the buildings in the Independence Mall National Historical Park. Each wing is treated in parallel fashion by the architect so that balance, harmony, logicality, and taste are all apparent. For instance, the President is the chief executive, while the Supreme Court is the chief judiciary. Eligibility requirements are spelled out for each branch. The issue of impeachment is raised in the respective articles rather than integrated into one article. The structure is on a grand scale and it ingeniously links quite different dimensions of government. The relationship of legislative, executive, and judicial powers is a brilliant achievement of imagination. This is not a deduction from principles or an inference from practice. The preamble, to continue our architectural paradigm, is the necessary entrance hall. A rear entrance is provided for future service by amendment (Article 5). Article 4 on the states might be thought of as another floor. The basement remained to be finished by the Bill of Rights. Article 6 is a miscellany that does not fit well. Article 7, on ratification, is that final signing with the contractor whereby one takes possession of the edifice one has designed. The architectonics of the Constitution as a composition are remarkable for their clarity of line and economy of presentation. The Constitution's main outlines, ordered in a mere seven articles, have imposing grace.

Aesthetics tips us off to the presence of themes or motifs in texts. One prominent theme in the Constitution is impeachment. How embarrassing to repeatedly refer to failings anticipated in the new order one is creating! Yet these are human failings, and the Constitution does not pretend to change human nature. Instead, it proposes forms and procedures which protect the people against abuses that we naturally fall victim to. The impeachment structure is part of the inventiveness that we may admire, while the mention of impeachment is a sober caution to the weak-natured.

The overriding theme of the Constitution is corrigibility. The check of one wing upon another can be understood as a mode of correction. And the mutual corrections seem never to end: the President may veto a bill, Congress may override the veto, the Supreme Court may strike down the law, the President appoints the Justices to the Supreme Court, Congress must concur in the appointment, and so on. Correction also comes about periodically through elections, but three different kinds of election and terms of office apply to Representatives, Senators, and the President. The

Constitution, moreover, carries its own method of corrigibility within it: the amendment article (Article 5). Thus, the Constitution is not a perfect text, nor does it presume a perfect world, but it opens itself to improvement.

The artistry of the Constitution is not carved in stone, but it has the flexibility and vitality of keeping up with the people in its history. Ours is a living Constitution. This is a case, known to aestheticians, where the audience contributes to the conception and shaping as well as to the appreciation of what they are offered. We perennially find in the Constitution a wording, a vision, a provision that speaks to our current needs. The Constitution in that sense continues to grow. It is not finished and enshrined like an artwork in a museum. It is still creatively active, or, as Morris Grossman puts it, still in performance. Hence, we are still creatively active as a people, insofar as we appreciate the Constitution. America has been a dance for two hundred years in which the people have had the Constitution as partner.

We are a young country but with the oldest written constitution in continuous use. We must understand the Constitution as our creation but we may also understand ourselves as in part the Constitution's creation. The Constitution has been the basic score for the American opera, the plot of our national destiny, the script for our dramatic enactment. Aesthetics is necessary here if we are to grasp the cultural force of the Constitution in the American identity, for mythic powers are at work. The Constitution and the Declaration of Independence, with which it is often confounded, are the equivalent for America of a national epic. They are our very own treasure that speaks our language, that is subject to memorization and recitation, and that continues to forge our identity as a people. The Declaration and the Constitution are our secular Scriptures: old testament and new testament. The Constitution is the final reference point, the rock-bottom commitment which binds us. Even the President, the commander in chief, must take an oath to protect and defend the Constitution as the first act upon taking office (Article 2, Section 1). No one is above the Constitution. The epithet, "That's unconstitutional!" is the strongest American denunciation. It is worse than "That's not kosher!"

As during the Bicentennial we look to the Constitution's intellectual contents and its political and legal significance, let us also keep an eye open, an aesthetically open eye, to the mythic, cultural, and creative uses of the Constitution. We shall find that the Constitution means an enormous amount to those, including the greater part of our compatriots, who have never read it.

UNDERSTANDING CONSTITUTIONAL RIGHTS: THE CONTRIBUTION OF PRAGMATIC PHILOSOPHY

Frederic R. Kellogg

The controversy over judicial activism is as old as the question whether law is "made" or "found" by the courts, and is the quintessential living question for legal philosophers. Here the practical meets the abstract, as Supreme Court justices must, explicitly or not, adopt some philosophical viewpoint in deciding how general constitutional propositions do, or do not, decide current concrete controversies.

The United States Constitution is not self-executing, but must be applied. But whence derives the legitimacy of nine men, distinguished only by their professional training as lawyers, in overruling the acts of a duly elected legislature, in a matter to which the document speaks only generally, and has been interpreted inconsistently? To answer that requires a firm sense of how courts can know what "law" is, its proper method of inquiry and analysis, and indeed how, if at all, "fundamental law" is interpreted and applied.

The dominant schools are at loggerheads over those issues. Legal positivism, characterized by the insistence that law and morals are separate, first prospered as a challenge to the sweeping enlightenment conceptions of law as divine or natural right, or deriving from social contract. To the deductive tendencies of natural law, to explain (and thereby control) the concrete through the general, Bentham and Austin offered a strict inductive prescription, defining law as only that actually commanded by the sovereign and rigidly excluding from the definition of law all notion of what it "ought to be."[1]

This position, skillfully maintained in this century by modern British scholars,[2] renewed American concern with explaining the legitimacy of Supreme Court authority over duly adopted rules and statutes which, through deduction, appeared offensive to fundamental rights. A temporal confidence that this explanation could be accomplished by identifying commonly accepted precepts of jurisprudential norms[3] or process[4] was shattered by the combination of rekindled legal realism with Derridean attacks upon the textual capriciousness of judicial review.[5] Thus was born Critical Legal Studies, challenging all but raw political explanations of judicial decision making.

Oliver Wendell Holmes, Jr., ranks high among proponents of constitutional restraint, his pronouncements having been approved by the respected realist academics during his Supreme Court tenure. Holmes' own philosophy remains a subject of wide disagreement,[6] but he is presented here as a legal pragmaticist. While legal realism had pragmatic associations,[7] it was influenced more by empiricist behaviorism than critical conceptualism of early pragmatists. Holmes, however, dissociated his own philosophy from both Peirce[8] and James,[9] although acknowledging early influence from Chauncey Wright[10] and later admiration for Dewey.[11] Only recently has his constitutional restraint been linked to pragmatic methodology.[12]

The theory which underlies such famous Holmes opinions as the dissent in *Lochner v. New York*[13] marks a highly original approach to the questions addressed by positivism, natural law, and process jurisprudence, and one which should survive the challenge of critical legal scholarship. In *Lochner* the proper method of constitutional analysis is neither deductive nor inductive, but closer to the "abduction" of Peirce or the "instrumentalism" or "experimentalism" of Dewey. General legal concepts are defined and limited by their *operations*, in historical context, and the law is a system of inquiry. Constitutional rights are not fixed *a priori* propositions which decide concrete cases in advance, but approximations accommodating prior experience with future consequences. In this respect they are fundamentally like common law rules, defining causes of action and focusing inquiry.[14]

The issue in *Lochner* was whether state legislation, restricting the hours that private businesses could contract with bakers to work, violated the right of free contract, thought to fall within the constitutional guaranty that "No State shall . . . deprive any citizen of life, liberty, or property, without due process of law." A majority, expressing the fear that one restriction on working conditions would inevitably lead to others,[15] held the act unconstitutional as imposing on unfettered contractual freedom.

Holmes, in dissent, commented that "The 14th amendment does not enact Mr. Herbert Spencer's *Social Statics*," and noted that innumerable other examples of state laws infringing absolute freedom of contract had been accepted, such as regulation of securities and unfair competition. He observed that "a Constitution is not intended to embody a particular economic theory, whether of paternalism and the organic relation of the citizen to the state or of laissez faire."[16] Two important elements of pragmatic method, insofar as it can be identified in writings of Peirce and Dewey roughly contemporary to Holmes,[17] are clearly contained in this opinion. These are the principle of limitation of general concepts to the particulars which have previously warranted their use, and the caution against extending their meaning by importing sweeping explanatory metaphysical (read "philosophical") systems, no matter how widely accepted.

The first is essentially Peirce's classic statement of pragmatic rule, "Consider what effects, that might conceivably have practical bearings, we conceive the object of our conception to have. Then, our conception of these effects is the whole of our conception of the object." (5.402) This is applied in law through the rigorous comparison of the implications of the concept (infringement of free contract) in the case at hand (baker's working hours) with the operation of the concept in previously settled applications (regulations of securities and unfair competition, as examples of prior cases).

The second element is contained in Holmes' statement that the fourteenth amendment does not enact Spencer's social Darwinism, which he explains with the comment that a Constitution is not intended to embody a particular economic theory. The pragmatic derivation of this may be elucidated in an extraordinary parallel between an early Holmes article on possession[18] and a later one by Dewey on corporate personality (one of his few writings on law) nearly fifty years later.[19] In both, the authors demonstrate how legal treatise-writers were importing deontological notions from Kantian philosophy into technical legal concepts like possession and personality, carrying them far astray from actual legal precedent.[20]

Neither of these articles addressed the subject of "fundamental" or constitutional principles, but rather general legal categories taken from a context of common (traditional, court-shaped) and statutory law. It was not until his elevation to the Supreme Judicial Court of Massachusetts in 1882 that Holmes had occasion to apply constitutional concepts. His earlier writings left the subject practically unattended, but laid a theoretical foundation for treating constitutional law according to the same theoretical scheme.

In his early essays and classic treatise, *The Common Law*, Holmes showed how seeing law as inquiry clarifies the use of concepts like rights. Although stated in the absolute, rights are like all general legal proscriptions in being *unsettled*. Even constitutional rights are "in fact limited by the neighborhood of principles of policy which are other than those on which the particular right is founded."[21] The right of free speech, for example, while declaring itself "absolute to [its] logical extreme,"[22] will not tolerate shouting "fire" in a crowded theater.[23] In a case wherein the disputed speech falls somewhat short of that, a judgment must be made, which is not enlightened by the categorical proposition itself. The right focuses the inquiry, but does not resolve it.

While this may seem evident enough upon reflection, Holmes found an endemic failure to recognize it among the judges and writers of his time, when it came to resolving conflicts between constitutional claims with statutory and common law. The *Lochner* case provides an illustrative example. When the constitutional right is placed in the balance with state legislation inimical to the judges' opinions, its putative "absolute" nature provides a ready, but false, rationale for overthrowing the entire state scheme on final, unreviewable, constitutional grounds. Thus the main thrust of pragmatic method in Holmes' thought lay in guarding against unchecked reign to political or ideological biases among the judges.

Holmes was every bit as aware of critical legal scholars of the indeterminacy of constitutional propositions; his own critical legal maxim, contained within the *Lochner* dissent, was: "general propositions do not decide concrete cases." The illusion that they did was supplied, or fueled, by the very notion which Holmes and Dewey challenged in their respective articles on possession and personality: that general legal concepts permitted the importation of doctrine or logical structure from external philosophical theories or systems.

But in stripping away this false determinacy Holmes did not arrive with the critical legal scholars at a perspective from which all constitutional review was unredeemably political. That was, for Holmes, certainly no more the case than non-constitutional judicial interpretation of statutes, or indeed judicial creation and modification of general common law rules and principles. Inquiry under constitutional jurisdiction was founded upon essentially the same legitimate basis as the common law.

The pragmatic meaning of a right was not so much the power of the protective sweep of an absolute expression or proposition, but the power to initiate public, objective, formal inquiry. The outcome would then depend upon the facts of the individual case, guided analogically by the experience of prior cases as well as the present sense of the impact of the requested ruling upon future cases and conduct. A general, abstract right, such as the right to constitutional due process or the first amendment right to free expression, is at heart a statement of jurisdiction, like the common law jurisdiction over claims of negligence. Such jurisdiction does not contain the power to decide abstract questions, but concrete controversies.

Rather than taking this reductive approach to constitutional theory and jurisdiction, critical legal scholarship instead launches an all-out attack on the *expansive* approach to constitutional jurisdiction which has gained the mainstream among post-realist American scholarship. The expansive approach, in turn, has been adopted by mainstream scholars as a necessary foundation to justify the fact that the United States Supreme Court has indeed appeared to decide abstract questions under constitutional jurisdiction--not so much now in the economic sphere like the *Lochner* court, but in civil and human rights.

Although sympathetic with many of the actual decisions, the critical legal scholars (along with neo-conservatives; philosophy makes for strange bedfellows) see them as examples of judicial policymaking and deny their legitimacy. They assert that in order for constitutional review to occur, meaning must be given by an interpreter, who necessarily reads the document against a particular social and political environment. There are no neutral standards which yield consistent results regardless of the values of the interpreter applying them. Hence Supreme Court interpretations of the Constitution reflect little more than judicial enforcement of value choices already made in the existing order.[24] Thus we find a leading CLS scholar adopting the position that "constitutional review is necessary but impossible."

The view that law is simply another form of policy created by unrepresentative judges is not new, nor confined to discussion of constitutional law. It was first advanced in this century by the legal realists; the major change of emphasis of critical scholars has been to shift criticism from a behavioral to a conceptual basis. Exemplifying this is their abandonment of what they have called the "trivial interest" criticism": that a judge's decisions are guided by individual behavioral criteria, including social background, class, income, character, and rules are simply chosen as rationalizations of a decision already predetermined by these.

Instead, the new critical scholars emphasize the incoherence of underlying legal-political theory. Whereas the earlier realist critique suggested the possibility of behavioral understanding leading to reform, the new criticism does not believe that reform is possible. Hence the characterization that critical scholarship "delegitimates" judicial review: the system cannot work as conventional theorists maintain, even if all of the actors are perfectly benevolent and capable of neutralizing their social class biases. These delegitimizers assert that the interpretations which the legal system seeks to enforce simply have no basis outside the systematic biases of society.[25]

Thus the CLS position accepts the assumption underlying its adversaries' position: that the Constitution grants the power to decide abstract questions, rather than only concrete controversies. Amidst the bitter controversy it goes unnoticed that this very assumption is challenged by legal pragmatism.

The question put by the critical legal scholars, whether the general language of constitutional rights (or any formula designed to elucidate them) may be relied on to decide a particular controversy, would for Holmes undoubtedly have had a negative answer--but the question itself is the wrong one. Centuries of experience under the common law had demonstrated that this is not the manner in which context and meaning is given to law. This message lay at the core of Holmes' scholarship prior to 1881. The fact that a negative answer is given by history to that question, as regards common law rights, could not mean for him that judicial decisions are fundamentally illegitimate.

Both CLS and the mainstream of American scholarship assume that constitutional jurisdiction is somehow different from other forms of judicial jurisdiction which have grown up over the ages, like Holmes' own favorite example: common law negligence. Nothing contained within the concept of negligence itself, nor the judicial tests for its application, suffice to decide a given case. Hence it can equally be said of negligence that "there are no neutral standards which yield consistent results regardless of the interpreter applying them." Yet meaning has gradually been given to negligence by the decision of particular cases:

> It is the merit of the common law that it decides the case first and determines the principle afterwards. Looking at the forms of logic it might be inferred that when you have a minor premise and a conclusion, there must be a major, which you are also prepared then and there to assert. It is only after a series of determinations on the same subject matter that it becomes necessary to "reconcile the cases," as it is called, that is, by a true induction to state the principle which has until then been obscurely felt. And this statement is often modified more than once by new decisions before the abstracted general rule takes its final shape. A well-settled legal doctrine embodies the work of many minds, and has been tested in form as well as in substance by trained critics whose practical interest it is to resist it at every step.[26]

Holmes' pragmatic orientation eventually led him to a conception of the judicial power devolving from constitutional rights as a power to inquire into certain limited issues raised by governmental activity, rather than a "power to decide" broad issues of policy once and for all. In effect, the Constitution could legitimately be interpreted to provide a special set of judicial causes of action, consistent in nature with those of the common law, but severely limited by constraints of legislative supremacy and common law precedent which he gradually worked out over a half-century judicial career.[27] The key to their proper application was the recognition that the power to decide was not coextensive with the breadth of constitutional language.

It is in the notion of an unlimited "power to decide" all matters logically within the scope of broad constitutional rights such as "liberty" and "due process" that the modern theory of constitutional jurisdiction has gone astray, carrying its critics along with it. The encompassing scope of the language of due process and the notion of constitutional "right" forced Holmes to reject the notion that whenever a logically plausible claim of violation was pressed on the Court, it had the power to decide the matter either way. Indeed, where an equally plausible legislative determination had been made to the contrary (assuming the legislature had actually addressed the issue in controversy), the Constitution could not be read to present a countervailing principle to be placed in a judicial balance scale. The same was true of common law precedent.

To hold otherwise was to create a general power for federal courts to reconsider and overrule legislation and state court decision, like a supreme appeals court of general jurisdiction. Abstention was required not by a mere "policy" of judicial restraint, which amounted to little more than a cautionary admonition. It was required by an understanding of the nature of constitutional law, in turn required by Holmes' fundamental principles of legal philosophy. There is no metaphysical essence to constitutional law, somehow enveloping all urgent controversies and providing a given outcome with the sanctity of rightness, simply because the controversy could be argued within the context of a constitutional "right."

For this reason, a threshold aspect of constitutional inquiry was the jurisdictional determination itself. If the matter was already governed by a definitive expression of consensus, abstention was required. Assuming that a truly "fundamental" aspect of the constitutional scheme was at stake, the Court must first determine that no consensus already occupied the field, and in the degree to which the facts presented the initial stage of a new and original controversy, it must be careful only to decide the specific case, so as not to foreclose further exploration--by the lower courts and the people's elected representatives--by sweeping opinions resolving the general matter once and for all.

The challenge of critical legal scholarship to the legitimacy of constitutional review ignores the jurisdictional issue, and instead launches a compelling attack on the *implications* of assuming that the power to decide follows the broad constitutional language, rather than the assumption itself. The attack seems far more persuasive than it is, because it addresses a position which in Holmes' conceptualization is a fallacy: the notion that the Constitution creates a power to decide wherever its language provides plausible reach.

The CLS position accepts the expansive "power-to-decide" conception of jurisdiction when it claims, as does Mark Tushnet, that "constitutional review is both necessary and impossible." What is *impossible* is any justification for the broad scope of the alleged necessity implied by the modern conception of jurisdiction. What *is* possible is that which the common law has ordained for centuries, but in a constitutional context: case-by-case inquiry into the controversies which place at issue the traditional liberties guaranteed by the Constitution, without trammeling the consensus already embodied in common law precedent and legislative action, or prematurely foreclosing its development. To be sure, this is a doctrine of severe judicial restraint; but it is the only approach which may overcome the problems encountered by modern constitutional scholarship.

NOTES

1. See generally F. Kellogg, *The Formative Essays of Justice Holmes*. (Westport: Greenwood Press, 1984), pp. 3-22.

2. See, e.g., H.L.A. Hart, *The Concept of Law*. (Oxford: Clarendon Press, 1961).

3. See, e.g., H. Wechsler, "Toward Neutral Principles of Constitutional Law," *Harvard Law Review*, vol. 73 (1959), p. 1.

4. See, e.g., H. Hart and A. Sacks, *The Legal Process: Basic Problems in the Making and Application of Law*. (tent. ed. 1958).

5. See, e.g., Note, "Round and Round the Bramble Bush: From Legal Realism to Critical Legal Scholarship," *Harvard Law Review*, vol. 95 (1982), p. 1669.

6. See, e.g., G. Edward White, "Looking at Holmes in the Mirror," *Law and History Review*, vol. 4 (1985-86), p. 439.

7. See F. Kellogg, supra n. 1, at p. 71, n. 40.

8. O. W. Holmes to Harold Laski, November 29, 1923, in M. Howe, *Holmes-Laski Letters*, vol. 2. (Cambridge MA: Harvard University Press, 1953), p. 565.

9. Holmes to Frederick Pollock, August 9, 1897, in M. Howe, *Holmes-Pollock Letters*, vol. 1. (Cambridge MA: Harvard University Press, 1946), p. 78.

10. Holmes to Pollock, August 30, 1929, *ibid*, vol. 2, p. 252.

11. Holmes to Pollock, May 15, 1931, *ibid.*, vol. 2, p. 287.

12. F. Kellogg, supra n. 1, pp. 3-74.

13. 198 U.S. 35, 75 (1904).

14. F. Kellogg, supra n. 1, p. 47.

15. 198 U.S. 35, 64.

16. Id. at p. 75-76.

17. See C.S. Peirce, "The Fixation of Belief" and "How to Make Our Ideas Clear," in *Collected Papers*. (Cambridge MA: Harvard University Press, 1978), 5.358-410; Dewey, "The Historical Background of Corporate Personality," *Yale Law Journal*, vol. 35 (1925-6), pp. 660-61.

18. Holmes, "Possession," *American Law Review*, vol. 12 (July, 1878), p. 688, reprinted in Kellogg, supra n. 1, p. 167.

19. Dewey, supra n. 17.

20. Holmes, supra n. 18, p. 701; Dewey, supra n. 17, p. 659.

21. *Hudson Cty. Water Co. v. McCarter*, 209 U.S. 349, 355 (1908).

22. See, e.g., id. at p. 355: "All rights tend to declare themselves absolute to their logical extreme."

23. *Schenck v. United States*, 249 U.S. 47, 52 (1918).

24. M. Tushnet, "Darkness on the Edge of Town: The Contribution of John Hart Ely to Constitutional Theory," *Yale Law Journal*, vol. 89 (May, 1980), p. 1037.

25. Id.; S. Carter, "Constitutional Adjudication and the Indeterminate Text: A Preliminary Defense of the Imperfect Muddle," *Yale Law Journal*, vol. 94 (March, 1985), p. 824-25 and citations.

26. Holmes, "Codes, and the Arrangement of Law," *American Law Review*, vol. 5 (October, 1870), p. 1, reprinted in Kellogg, supra n. 1, p. 77.

27. See Kellogg, "Common Law and Constitutional Theory: The Common Law Origins of Holmes' Constitutional Restraint," *George Mason Law Review*, vol. 7 (Fall, 1984), p. 177.

CONSTITUTION, HOLMES AND CRITICS: COMMENTARY ON F. KELLOGG

Christopher B. Gray

Kellogg's main claim is that pragmatic case-by-case inquiry is "the only approach to overcome the problems encountered by modern constitutional scholarship." This claim involves three others, about the United States Constitution, about Oliver Wendell Holmes, Jr., and about Critical Legal Studies.

These further claims are that the Constitution can be interpreted rightly only by a pragmatic method; that Holmes developed and used such a constitutional method; and that the Critics do not, making their studies beside the point.

Pragmatic method is defined in the paper by two principles. First, general concepts are limited to the particulars which have previously warranted their use. The second principle is that the conception of the effects makes up the whole conception of the object.

Restating the three claims about Holmes, Constitution and Critics in terms of the two pragmatic principles, the Constitution is not an open-ended grant of jurisdictional power, but grants power only to decide singular cases. Holmes expressed and used a method of attention to singular cases and their results. And the Critics err by taking the Constitution as such an open-ended grant; their conclusion that law's indeterminacy is parasitic on political power does not follow.

Constitution

We must start naively and ask why the judicial power is not to be considered open-ended when it looks that way. Parallel to the grants of legislative and executive power, "the judicial power of the United States shall be vested in one Supreme Court . . . ." (Article III, Section 1) "The judicial power shall extend to all cases . . . arising under this Constitution." (Subsection 2(1)) "This Constitution" involves identifying over singular cases what are the justice and tranquility, and the welfare and liberty in its preamble, but also what are the respective numbers or the republican government or the supreme law in its body, as well as the freedom, due process and equal protection in its amendments. This naivete needs some reason why it should not prevail.

Looking to the Constitution's pervasive "democratic" ethos, lest nine old WASPs dominate the people's elected representatives, begs the question of why its implicit ethos, if such there is, forbids this when its explicit statements seem to provide for just that. Instead, the open-ended grant of jurisdictional power is denied because constitutional rights define causes of action, and focus inquiry, like the common law. So we must determine the decisions by common law methods, by pragmatic methods.

But whether constitutional law is common law may be questioned. Constitutional law does not arise like common law. Common law arises initially out of procedural writs, and continues to arise thereafter on previously decided cases as well. No preexisting principles serve either as content or criteria for claims that are made in the cases.

This is not true of constitutional law. Under a written constitution, the law arises out of a statute-like instrument which does lay out content and criteria to confine decisions. Simply because it does not do so fully is no reason to say it does not do so simply. There is a world of difference between starting with a historical feature of, e.g., possession which can be distinguished away, and starting from a requirement for, e.g., equality which can only be escaped but never dismissed.

In this respect, constitutions are like codes, rather than common law. But Holmes was allergic to codes from the start. Since Holmes reduced any code to no more than using the courts' words, why not cut out the middleman and just stick to the courts' own words? The only other thing a code could do is attempt to anticipate the governing process, which he would "not dwell on . . ., as its possible import is small." Secondly, even if a code were in place, cases would soon elude it. Then these cases must be cut down onto its codal bed frame, or must be decided beyond the code, making it a statement of the *ratio juris* only, not law but a textbook.[1]

Holmes' prejudgment is remarkable since he even notes the near-at-hand counterexample of the Quebec (called "Canadian") Civil Code. What Holmes excludes is precisely what codes are intended to do, and do: to anticipate the governing process, indeed, thereby directing it; and to state that, right within the law, rather than only implicit, or only outside of it in "textbooks", lies an explicit intelligibility. Thus of codes; even more of code-like instruments that are written constitutions, whose intent is precisely to anticipate the governance, and to state the values which direct it.

Though the common law and the written constitution do not start out alike, perhaps Holmes bridges from one to the other, and so proves their continuity under pragmatic method. The bridge would have to be his essay on "Early English Equity" where he studies the ancestor of the trust.[2] The term "equity" even now connotes the mandate to achieve some set of general values, just as does a constitution, and as it denotes in civilian law. Not surprisingly, it is this connotation Holmes is at pains to explode.

His argument is that the common law courts could have protected the beneficiary but for a historical accident; that, instead, the trustee (to use here yet another anachronistic term) was substantively modelled on a Teutonic institution; and so the Chancery's additions to the common law were merely procedural. The gist is that no general value is added to common law by equity. A cognate conclusion can be drawn, then, about constitutional law. But the historical key to his argument is not something of which "there can be no doubt." For scholars who have reexamined this history[3] instead of merely following Holmes' authority,[4] have found it to be untrue.

Holmes' scholarship has as its end to assimilate all law into his conception of the common law, law as one-by-one experimental attention to singular facts with no preconceptions. We may be permitted to refuse his invitation to assimilate constitutional law, when we see how he tortures into it the related area of equity, which might have bridged to the written constitution.

If pragmatic method is not authorized for constitutional interpretation because of being native to the common law, is the common law method perhaps required because it is pragmatic? Is there some reason for Holmes to insist directly upon pragmatic method for the U.S. Constitution?

Not that it is an intrinsic attribute of any document to be interpreted pragmatically, for that is a non-pragmatic essential definition. Instead, a definition by consequences would look for the enhanced external relations between parties to a document of this type. The U.S. Constitution is of a legal type, an authoritative writing. What, then, authorizes its pragmatic interpretation?

Authority may come from the Framers; but they must first escape from non-originist critiques. Or the text itself may allow for reconsideration of some facts, like regular recounts of slaves (Article I, Subsection 2(3)); for some experiments, as by amendment (Article V); for an emergence of new rights' consciousness (Articles IX-X). But this is weak brew in terms of what is needed for a pragmatic mandate.

If not the authors nor text, the cases may authorize the method. Are constitutional decisions pragmatic, because being so makes them better decisions?[5]

Holmes' Decisions

Can we see that Holmes' own cases were pragmatically decided and, if so, that their results were superior? What needs to be determined is whether the two features of the method identified earlier are present in Holmes' decisions: attending closely to the factual outcomes of actions; and importing no general theory. But both are missing: Holmes pays little attention to factual outcomes; and he does import general theory. *Lochner* can illustrate both failures.

The generality Holmes rejected in *Lochner* was freedom of contract. The particular facts against it were the restrictions upon freedom of action and of contract which the courts and legislatures had allowed.[6] Yet what do they show? Not that there is no freedom of contract, another generality, but only that freedom of contract has counterexamples. Do they disprove the generality, or make it useless as general? Not if the counterexamples are no more than exceptions to a generality which still holds, or are a competing generality's instances.

Where does Holmes leave the counterexamples? Are they exceptions to a rule? He does not say so, or give any other rationale for them. As they stand, all one can say is: sometimes there is freedom, sometimes there is not. Whether restricting bakery hours to ten a day is more akin to freedom-cases or non-freedom cases are the only factual consequences which would have helped a decision, and constituted an exercise of the method. But the comparison is not made.

Let us turn to the other branch of pragmatic method exemplified by *Lochner*: to import no general theory as a way of characterizing particulars. Holmes expunged laissez-faire theory, and also paternalist theory. But while expunging theory from law, he did not scour out generality. All he got rid of is a generality someone claims to be true and gives reasons for: a universality. But generality is allowed into law as long as it is opinion.

Good law holds "the right of a majority to embody their opinions in law." While a constitution is not intended to embody a *particular* economic theory, it is "made for people of fundamentally *different* views." Nothing should prevent "the natural outcome of a dominant opinion," that it become law. "Every opinion tends to become a law."[7]

The "proposition just stated" which "will carry us far toward" the decision (even if intuition must complete it) is not the famous sentence that "general propositions do not decide concrete cases." Rather, it is the paraphrased sentence, that "every opinion tends to become a law."

And the only limit upon the dominant role of general opinion in law, and its serving just as "theory" does, is another opinion only slightly less general, namely, "that a reasonable and fair man necessarily would admit that the statute proposed [by general opinion] would infringe fundamental principles as they have been understood by the traditions of our people and our law." General opinion penetrates the law, limited only by other general opinion.

Critics

As the third claim before this commentary, to defend legal determinacy against the legal studies critics, there may be other ways than by identifying a Holmesian pragmatism for dealing with the Constitution. Two steps can be taken: to critique their doctrinal basis in hermeneutical theory; and then, as they do, to examine their results. The self-negating character of continental hermeneutics, admitted by its practitioners and demonstrated as to law by Gillian Rose,[8] leaves no "reasons" or arguments driving one to that position, but only an invitation to change our perception, an invitation that will be accepted or declined, then, only upon its results.

As the Critics' results are set out by Altman and Wagner-DeCew,[9] the doctrinal incoherence in law occurs as contradiction not between rules at a relatively low level of abstraction (as various "mailbox" rules), nor between doctrines at the mid-level (like different requirements for consideration, or for reasonable reliance in contract law), but between ideals at the highest level (e.g., broad normative conceptions of the person). Though these necessarily express themselves in the doctrines and the rules, nonetheless because lower-level rules and doctrines are precedent-bound, "the law is by and large coherent. In (at least) the large majority of cases the pre-existing law dictates a single, determinate outcome."

If this is the outcome of the Critics' studies, perhaps their suggested resolution of the "irreconcilable conflict" at the highest level is suitable: that only *some* broad normative concepts are part of the law--not *all*, as in natural law; nor *none*, as in legal positivism--but those which fit legal doctrine both logically and culturally. These are logically generated from the nonconflictual legal doctrine, and are a significant part of our culture's normative framework.[10]

The Critics' objections are resolved by determinacy at the level of concrete singular case decisions. That should be enough to leave both the Critic and the pragmatist content. If so, pragmatizing Holmes and rendering the Constitution common law may be unnecessary.

NOTES

1. Frederic Rogers Kellogg, *The Formative Essays of Justice Holmes* [1870-80]; *The Making of an American Legal Philosophy.* (Westport CT: Greenwood Press, 1984), pp. 77-78.

2. Oliver Wendell Holmes, Jr., *Collected Legal Papers* [1885-1918]. (New York: Harcourt, Brace, 1921), esp. pp. 4-16. This 1885 essay was written ten years after ending *The Common Law* which summed up his early research, and two years after joining the Massachusetts bench on which constitutional questions first came to preoccupy him; but before any constitutional cases worth reproducing had reached him, in the view of his editor for this two year period when Holmes, nonetheless, wrote some eighty-two opinions: Harry C. Shriver, ed., *The Judicial Opinions of Oliver Wendell Holmes: Constitutional Opinions ... in the Supreme Judicial Court of Massachusetts* (1883-1902). (Buffalo: Dennis Co., 1940). As well, this essay is his only one on equity but for the essays on "Agency" from 1891.

3. J.L. Burton, "The Medieval Use," *Law Quarterly Review 11* (1965) 562-3; J.B. Ames, *Lecture on Legal History* (Cambridge: Harvard University Press, 1913), p. 237.

4. F. Pollock and F.W. Maitland, *The History of English Law Before the Time of Edward I*, 2 vols., 2d ed. (Cambridge University Press, 1923), I, p. 229, n. 1; A. Badre, *Le développement historique des "uses" jusqu'à l'introduction du trust en droit anglais.* (Paris: Rousseau, 1932), pp. 22-27; Theodore T.F. Plucknett, *A Concise History of the Common Law*, 4th ed. rev. (London: Butterworth, 1948), p. 545, n. 1.

5. To chasten this argument, it must be recalled that any decision can be reached by a variety of methods, and so it will certify none. Peirce provided at least four to "fix belief," of which the pragmatic was but one. Every concurring opinion written demonstrates that the legal decision is no exception.

6. Alfred Leif, ed., *The Dissenting Opinions of Mr Justice Holmes* [U.S. Supreme Court, 1903-27]. (New York: Vanguard Press, 1929), p. 2f.

7. *Ibid.*, my emphasis.

8. *Dialectic of Nihilism; Post-Structuralism and Law.* (Basil Blackwell, 1984).

9. Andrew Altman, "Legal Realism and Critical Legal Studies in Dworkin," *Philosophy and Public Affairs* 15 (1986)205, cited in his "Critical Legal Studies and the Incoherence of Law," paper at American Philosophical Association Eastern Conference, Boston, 1986; and commentary by Judith Wagner-DeCew, "Critical Legal Studies' Incoherence Thesis."

10. This is derivative from R. Dworkin, *Law's Empire*. (Harvard University Press, 1985).

THE U.S. CONSTITUTION: A FUNDAMENTALLY FLAWED DOCUMENT

James P. Sterba

The fundamental strength of the U.S. Constitution is that it guarantees rights to religious and political liberty. Its fundamental weakness is that it fails to guarantee rights to equal opportunity and welfare. That the U.S. Constitution fails to guarantee rights to equal opportunity and welfare seems clear enough. If we focus by way of example on educational opportunity, a majority of the Supreme Court determined in *San Antonio School District v. Rodriguez* (1973) that there is no constitutional right to education. In this case, the issue before the Supreme Court of the United States was whether the Texas School System, by making the availability of funds to school districts a function of the taxable wealth in those districts, is in violation of the Fourteenth Amendment requirement that all citizens receive "equal protection of the law." The majority of the Court held that since education is not a right afforded strict protection by the Federal Constitution and since the absolute deprivation of education is not at stake, the Texas School System is not in violation of the Fourteenth Amendment. Even in the *Brown v. Board of Education* decisions (1954, 1955) the Supreme Court did not recognize a constitutional right to education. Rather the Court declared that where the state has undertaken to provide educational opportunity, that opportunity must be made available to all on equal terms.

Thus, according to the Court, whatever right to education exists is conditional upon a state's decision to provide that opportunity; it is not a constitutional requirement.

The situation is quite similar with respect to welfare. In *Wyman v. James* (1971), the issue before the Supreme Court of the United States was whether the Fourth Amendment prohibition of unreasonable searches applies to visits by welfare caseworkers to recipients of the program for Aid to Families with Dependent Children. The majority of the Court held that the Fourth Amendment does not apply in this case because the visitation is not forced or compelled since one can avoid the visitation by choosing not to accept the aid. What one cannot choose to do is to receive the aid but forego the visitation, and that is because there is no constitutional right to welfare. The only right to welfare is a right that is conditional upon the state or federal government's interest in providing welfare, and presently that interest requires the acceptance of a home visitation.

Yet one might ask why should the failure to guarantee rights to equal opportunity and welfare render the U.S. Constitution a fundamentally flawed document? The reason for this, I claim, is that these rights can be shown to follow from a wide range of opposing contemporary moral and political ideals. In particular, I have argued that when correctly interpreted, these rights can be seen to follow from a Libertarian Ideal of Liberty, a Welfare Liberal Ideal of Contractual Fairness, a Communitarian Ideal of the Common Good, a Feminist Ideal of Androgyny and a Socialist Ideal of Equality. Consequently, if I am right that all these ideals, when correctly interpreted, require rights to equal opportunity and welfare, then surely these rights would have to be guaranteed by any constitution that claims to be morally defensible.

But are these rights really required by each of these five ideals? Certainly no one would deny that these rights are required by a Welfare Liberal Ideal of Contractual Fairness, assuming that the ideal is interpreted, as John Rawls has proposed, to involve hypothetical choice from behind a veil of ignorance that is thick enough to secure impartiality but thin enough to make unanimous agreement possible. This is because even if Rawls' critics are correct in claiming that persons behind such a veil of ignorance would not seek to maximize the payoffs to the least advantaged in society, it is certainly the case that persons so situated would favor rights to equal opportunity and welfare. Nevertheless, many would surely want to deny that these rights are also required by one or another of the other four ideals.

Now I do not have the space here to argue that all five of these ideals require rights to equal opportunity and welfare.[1] To make my case, I will simply argue that two of the five, a Libertarian Ideal of Liberty and a Communitarian Ideal of Common Good, when correctly interpreted, can be seen to require the same rights to equal opportunity and welfare that are required by a welfare liberal ideal. Yet although this argument is weaker than the fuller argument I have developed elsewhere, I think that it will still suffice to establish my claim that the U.S. Constitution is a fundamentally flawed document because it fails to guarantee rights to equal opportunity and welfare.

The Libertarian Ideal of Liberty

Now the Libertarian Ideal of Liberty has been defended in basically two different ways. Some libertarians, following Herbert Spencer, have 1) taken a right to liberty as basic and 2) derived all other rights from this right to liberty. Other libertarians, following John Locke, have 1) taken a set of rights, including typically a right to life and a right to property, as basic and 2) defined liberty as the absence of constraints in the exercise of these rights. Now both groups of libertarians regard liberty as the ultimate political ideal, but they do so for different reasons. For Spencerian Libertarians, liberty is the ultimate political ideal because all other rights are derived from a right to liberty. For Lockean Libertarians, liberty is the ultimate political ideal because liberty just is the absence of constraints in the exercise of people's fundamental rights.[2]

Spencerian Libertarians

Let us begin by considering the view of those libertarians who take a right to liberty to be basic and define all other rights in terms of this right to liberty. According to this view, liberty is usually interpreted as follows:

> *The Want Interpretation of Liberty*: Liberty is being unconstrained by other persons from doing what one wants.

Now this interpretation limits the scope of liberty in two ways. First, not all constraints whatever their source count as a restriction of liberty; the constraints must come from other persons. For example, people who are constrained from getting to the top of Mount Everest do not lack liberty in this regard. Second, constraints that have their source in other persons, but that do not run counter to an individual's wants, constrain without restricting that individual's liberty. Thus, for people who do not want to hear Beethoven's Fifth Symphony, the fact that others have effectively proscribed its performance does not restrict their liberty, even though it does constrain what they are able to do.

Of course, libertarians may wish to argue that even such constraints can be seen to restrict a person's liberty once we take into account the fact that people normally want, or have a general desire, to be unconstrained by others. But other philosophers have thought that the possibility of such constraints points to a serious defect in this conception of liberty,[3] which can only be remedied by adopting the following broader interpretation of liberty:

> *The Ability Interpretion of Liberty*: Liberty is being unconstrained by other persons from doing what one is able to do.

Applying this interpretation to the above example, we find that people's liberty to hear Beethoven's Fifth Symphony would be restricted even if they did not want to hear it (and even if, perchance, they did not want to be unconstrained by others) since other people would still be constraining them from doing what they are able to do.

Yet even if we accept all the liberties specified by the Ability Interpretation, we still need to decide what is to count as a constraint. On the one hand, libertarians would like to limit constraints to positive act (i.e., acts of commission) that prevent people from doing what they are otherwise able to do. On the other hand, welfare liberals and socialists interpret constraints to include, in addition, negative acts (i.e., acts of omission) that prevent people from doing what they are otherwise able to do. In fact, this is one way to understand the debate between defenders of "negative liberty" and defenders of "positive liberty." For the defenders of negative liberty would seem to interpret constraints to include only positive acts of others that prevent people from doing what they otherwise are able to do, while defenders of positive liberty would seem to interpret constraints to include both positive and negative acts of others that prevent people from doing what they are otherwise able to do.[4]

Now suppose that we interpret constraints in the manner favored by libertarians to include only positive acts by others that prevent people from doing what they are otherwise able to do. Interpreting their ideal in this way, libertarians claim to derive a number of more specific requirements, in particular, a right to life, a right to freedom of speech, press and assembly, and a right to property.

Here it is important to observe that the libertarians' right to life is not a right to receive from others the goods and resources necessary for preserving one's life; it is simply a right not to be killed unjustly. Correspondingly, the libertarian's right to property is not a right to receive from others the goods and resources necessary for one's welfare, but rather a right to acquire goods and resources either by initial acquisitions or by voluntary agreements.

Of course, libertarians would allow that it would be nice of the rich to share their surplus resources with the poor. Nevertheless, according to libertarians, such acts of charity should not be coercively required. For this reason, libertarians are opposed to coercively supported welfare systems.

For a similar reason, libertarians are opposed to coercively supported equal opportunity programs. This is because the educational and job opportunities one has under a Libertarian Ideal of Liberty are usually a function of the property one controls, and since unequal property distributions are taken to be justified under a Libertarian Ideal of Liberty, unequal educational and job opportunities are also regarded as justified.

Lockean Libertarians

The same results with respect to welfare and equal opportunity obtain for those libertarians who take a set of rights, typically including a right to life and a right to property, as basic and then interpret liberty as follows:

> *The Rights Interpretation of Liberty*: Liberty is being unconstrained by other persons from doing what one has a right to do.

For according to this view, a right to life is simply a right not to be killed unjustly; it is not a right to receive the goods and resources necessary for preserving one's life. Correspondingly, a right to property is a right to acquire property either by initial acquisitions or by voluntary transactions; it is not a right to receive from others whatever goods and resources one needs to maintain oneself. Understanding a right to life and a right to property in this way, libertarians reject both coercively supported welfare and equal opportunity programs as violations of liberty.

Now in order to see why libertarians are mistaken about what their ideal requires, consider a typical conflict situation between the rich and the poor. In this conflict situation, the rich, of course, have more than enough resources to satisfy their basic needs. By contrast, the poor lack the resources to meet their most basic needs even though they have tried all the means available to them that libertarians regard as legitimate for acquiring such resources. Under circumstances like these, Spencerian Libertarians usually maintain that the rich should have the liberty to use their resources to satisfy their luxury needs if they so wish. Spencerian Libertarians recognize that this liberty might well be enjoyed at the expense of the satisfaction of the most basic needs of the poor; they just think that liberty always has priority over other political ideals, and since they assume that the liberty of the poor is not at stake in such conflict situations, it is easy for them to conclude that the rich should not be required to sacrifice their liberty so that the basic needs of the poor may be met.

Of course, Spencerian Libertarians would allow that it would be nice of the rich to share their surplus resources with the poor. Nevertheless, according to Spencerian Libertarians, such acts of charity are not required because the liberty of the poor is not thought to be at stake in such conflict situations.

In fact, however, the liberty of the poor is at stake in such conflict situations. What is at stake is the liberty of the poor to take from the surplus possessions of the rich what is necessary to satisfy their basic needs. When Spencerian Libertarians are brought to see that this is the case, they are genuinely surprised, one might even say rudely awakened, for they had not previously seen the conflict between the rich and the poor as a conflict of liberties.[5]

Now when the conflict between the rich and the poor is viewed as a conflict of liberties, we can either say that the rich should have the liberty to use their surplus resources for luxury purposes, or we can say that the poor should have the liberty to take from the rich what they require to meet their basic needs. If we choose one liberty, we must reject the other. What needs to be determined, therefore, is which liberty is morally preferable: the liberty of the rich or the liberty of the poor?

The "Ought" Implies "Can" Principle

I submit that the liberty of the poor, which is the liberty to take from the surplus resources of others what is required to meet one's basic needs, is morally preferable to the liberty of the rich, which is the liberty to use one's surplus resources for luxury purposes. To see that this is the case, we need only appeal to one of the most fundamental principles of morality, one that is common to all political perspectives, namely, the "ought" implies "can" principle. According to this principle, people are not morally required to do what they lack the power to do or what would involve so great a sacrifice that it would be unreasonable to ask them to perform such an action.[6]

For example, suppose I promised to attend a departmental meeting on Friday, but on Thursday I am involved in a serious car accident which puts me into a coma. Surely it is no longer the case that I ought to attend the meeting now that I lack the power to do so. Or suppose instead that on Thursday I develop a severe case of pneumonia for which I am hospitalized. Surely I could claim that I no longer ought to attend the meeting on the grounds that the risk to my health involved in attending is a sacrifice that it would be unreasonable to ask me to bear. In this latter case, the underlying rationale is that I cannot be morally required to sacrifice the satisfaction of my most fundamental interests so that others can satisfy their peripheral interests unless I have freely chosen to make such a sacrifice.

Now it seems clear that the poor have it within their power to relinquish such an important liberty as the liberty to take from the rich what they require to meet their basic needs. Nevertheless, it would be unreasonable to ask them to make so great a sacrifice. In the extreme case, it would involve asking the poor to sit back and starve to death. Of course, the poor may have no real alternative to relinquishing this liberty. To do anything else may involve worse consequences for themselves and their loved ones and may invite a painful death. Accordingly, we may expect that the poor would acquiesce, albeit unwillingly, to a political system that denied them the right to welfare supported by such a liberty, at the same time that we recognize that such a system imposed an unreasonable sacrifice upon the poor--a sacrifice that we could not morally blame the poor for trying to evade.[7] Analogously, we might expect that a woman whose life was threatened would submit to a rapist's demands, at the same time that we recognize the utter unreasonableness of those demands.

By contrast, it would not be unreasonable to ask the rich to sacrifice the liberty to meet some of their luxury needs so that the poor can have the liberty to meet their basic needs. Of course, we might expect that the rich for reasons of self-interest and past contribution might be disinclined to make such a sacrifice. We might even suppose that the past contribution of the rich provides a good reason for not sacrificing their liberty to use their surplus for luxury purposes. Yet, unlike the poor, the rich could not claim that relinquishing such a liberty involved so great a sacrifice that it would be unreasonable to ask them to make it; unlike the poor, the rich could be morally blameworthy for failing to make such a sacrifice.

Consequently, if we assume that however else we specify the requirements of morality, they cannot violate the "ought" implies "can" principle, it follows that, despite what Spencerian Libertarians claim, the right to liberty endorsed by them actually favors the liberty of the poor over the liberty of the rich.

Yet couldn't Spencerian Libertarians object to this conclusion, claiming that it would be unreasonable to ask the rich to sacrifice the liberty to meet some of their luxury needs so that the poor could have the liberty to meet their basic needs? As I have pointed out, Spencerian Libertarians do not usually see the situation as a conflict of liberties, but suppose they did. How plausible would such an objection be? Not very plausible at all, I think.

For consider: what are Spencerian Libertarians going to say about the poor? Is it not clearly unreasonable to ask the poor to sacrifice the liberty to meet their basic needs so that the rich can have the liberty to meet their luxury needs? Is it not clearly unreasonable to ask the poor to sit back and starve to death? If it is, then there is no resolution of this conflict that would be reasonable to ask both the rich and the poor to accept. But that would mean that the libertarian ideal of liberty cannot be a moral ideal; for a moral ideal resolves conflicts of interest in ways that it would be reasonable to ask everyone affected to accept. Therefore, as long as Spencerian Libertarians think of themselves as putting forth a moral ideal, they cannot allow that it would be unreasonable *both* to ask the rich to sacrifice the liberty to meet some of their luxury needs in order to benefit the poor and to ask the poor to sacrifice the liberty to meet their basic needs in order to benefit the rich. But I submit that if one of these requests is to be judged reasonable, then, by an neutral assessment, it must be the request that the rich sacrifice the liberty to meet some of their luxury needs so that the poor can have the liberty to meet their basic needs; there is no other plausible solution, if the Spencerian Libertarians intend to be putting forth a moral ideal.

Let us now consider the view of Lockean Libertarians, who take a set of rights, typically including a right to life and a right to property, as basic and then interpret liberty as being unconstrained by other persons from doing what one has a right to do. According to this view, a right to life is understood as a right not to be killed unjustly, and a right to property is understood as a right to acquire goods and resources either by initial acquisitions or voluntary transactions. Obviously, to evaluate this view, we need to determine what are the practical implications of these basic rights.

Presumably, a right to life understood as a right not to be killed unjustly would not be violated by defensive measures designed to protect one's person from life-threatening attacks. Yet would this right be violated when the rich prevent the poor from taking what they require to satisfy their basic needs? Obviously, as a consequence of such preventive actions poor people do sometimes starve to death. Have the rich, then, in contributing to this result, killed the poor, or simply let them die; and if they have killed the poor, have they done so unjustly?

Now sometimes the rich in preventing the poor from taking what they require to meet their basic needs would not in fact be killing the poor, but only causing them to be physically or mentally debilitated. Yet since such preventive acts involve resisting the life-preserving activities of the poor, when the poor do die as a consequence of such acts, it seems clear that the rich would be killing the poor, whether intentionally or unintentionally.

Of course, Lockean Libertarians would want to argue that such killing is simply a consequence of the legitimate exercise of property rights, and hence, not unjust. But to understand why Lockean Libertarians are mistaken in this regard, let us appeal again to that fundamental principle of morality, the "ought" implies "can" principle. In this context, the principle can be used to assess two opposing accounts of property rights. According to the first account, a right to property is *not* conditional upon whether other persons have sufficient opportunities and resources to satisfy their basic needs. This view holds that the initial acquisitions and voluntary transactions of some can leave others, through no fault of their own, dependent upon charity for the satisfaction of their most basic needs. By contrast, according to the second account, initial acquisitions and voluntary transactions can confer title of property on all goods and resources except those surplus goods and resources of the rich that are required to satisfy the basic needs of those poor who through no fault of their own lack the opportunities and resources to satisfy their own basic needs.

Clearly, only the first of these two accounts of property rights would generally justify the killing of the poor as a legitimate exercise of the property rights of the rich. Yet it would be unreasonable to ask the poor to accept anything other than some version of the second account of property rights.

Moreover, according to the second account, it does not matter whether the poor would actually die or are only physically or mentally debilitated as a result of such acts of prevention. Either result would preclude property rights from arising. Of course, the poor may have no real alternative to acquiescing to a political system modeled after the first account of property rights, even though such a system imposes an unreasonable sacrifice upon them--a sacrifice that we could not blame them for trying to evade. At the same time, although the rich would be disinclined to do so, it would not be unreasonable to ask them to accept a political system modeled after the second account of property rights--the account favored by the poor.

Consequently, if we assume that however else we specify the requirements of morality, they cannot violate the "ought" implies "can" principle, it follows that, despite what Lockean Libertarians claim, the right to life and the right to property endorsed by them actually support a right to welfare.

A Right to Equal Opportunity

By a similar argument which weighs the conflicting liberties or rights involved, it can be shown that an ideal of liberty also supports a right to equal opportunity. Now it is possible that libertarians convinced to some extent by the above arguments might want to accept a right to welfare and a right to the basic opportunities that are necessary for the satisfaction of one's basic needs but then deny that there is a right to equal opportunity. Such a stance, however, is only plausible if we restrict the class of morally legitimate claimants to those within a given (affluent) society for only then would a right to equal opportunity be different from the right to the basic opportunities necessary for the satisfaction of people's basic needs. But once it is recognized that the class of morally legitimate claimants includes distant peoples and future generations, then even libertarians should grant that guaranteeing the basic opportunities necessary for the satisfaction of their basic needs to all morally legitimate claimants would lead to providing them all with roughly equal opportunity.[8]

What these arguments show, therefore, is that a libertarian ideal supports the same practical requirements as a welfare liberal ideal. Both favor a right to welfare and a right to equal opportunity.

A Communitarian Ideal of the Common Good

Let us now consider a Communitarian Ideal of the Common Good. As one might expect, many contemporary defenders of a communitarian ideal regard their ideal as rooted in Aristotelian moral theory. Like Aristotle, they endorse a fundamental contrast between human beings as they are and human beings as they could be if they realize their essential nature. Ethics is then viewed as a science which enables human beings to understand how they make the transition from the former state to the latter. On this view, ethics requires some account of potency to act and some account of the essence of human beings and the telos or end which they seek. Moreover, for human beings to make this transition from potency to act, a particular set of virtues is needed. Human beings who fail to acquire these virtues thereby fail to realize their true nature and reach their true end.

While many contemporary defenders of a communitarian ideal accept these elements of Aristotelian moral theory, many also agree with Alasdair MacIntyre that if Aristotelian moral theory is to be rationally acceptable it must be refurbished in certain respects. Specifically, MacIntyre claims that Aristotelian moral theory must, first of all, reject any reliance on a metaphysical biology.[9] Instead of appealing to a metaphysical biology, MacIntyre proposes to ground Aristotelian moral theory on a conception of a practice. A practice, for MacIntyre, is "any coherent and complex form of socially established cooperative human activity through which goods internal to that form of activity are realized in the course of trying to achieve those standards of excellence which are appropriate to and partially definitive of that form of activity, with the result that human powers to achieve excellence, and human conceptions of the ends and goods involved are systematically extended."[10] As examples of practices, MacIntyre cites arts, sciences, games, and the making and sustaining of family life.[11]

MacIntyre then partially defines the virtues in terms of practices. A virtue, such as courage, justice or honesty, is "an acquired human quality the possession and exercise of which tends to enable us to achieve those goods which are internal to practices and the lack of which prevents us from achieving any such goods."[12] However, MacIntyre admits that the virtues which sustain practices can conflict (e.g., courage can conflict with justice) and that practices so defined are not themselves above moral criticism.[13]

Accordingly, to further ground the communitarian account, MacIntyre introduces the conception of a telos or good of a whole human life conceived as a unity.[14] It is by means of this conception that MacIntyre proposes to morally evaluate practices and resolve conflicts between virtues. For MacIntyre, the telos of a whole human life is a life spent in seeking that telos; it is a quest for the good human life and it proceeds with only partial knowledge of what is sought. Nevertheless, this quest is never undertaken in isolation but always within some shared tradition.[15] Moreover, such a tradition provides additional resources for evaluating practices and for resolving conflicts while remaining open to moral criticism itself.

MacIntyre's characterization of the human telos in terms of a quest undertaken within a tradition marks a second respect in which he wants to depart from Aristotle's view. This historical dimension to the human telos which MacIntyre contends is essential for a rationally acceptable communitarian account is absent from Aristotle's view.

A third respect in which MacIntyre's communitarian account departs from Aristotle's concerns the possibility of tragic moral conflicts.[16] As MacIntyre points out, Aristotle only recognized moral conflicts that are the outcome of wrongful or mistaken action. Yet MacIntyre, following Sophocles, wants to recognize the possibility of additional conflicts between rival moral goods that are rooted in the very nature of things. At the same time, MacIntyre wants to distinguish choice between such rival moral goods from choice between incommensurable premises.[17] According to MacIntyre, the difference is that choice of one rival good does "nothing to diminish or derogate" from the claims of the other upon the agent. The tragic chooser must simply recognize that she cannot do everything that she ought to do.

By refurbishing Aristotle's view in these ways, MacIntyre hopes to avoid the radical disagreement, interminable arguments and incommensurable premises which he claims characterize contemporary moral philosophy.[18] These three features, MacIntyre claims, are illustrated in the current debate between Robert Nozick and John Rawls.[19] Thus Nozick argues for the libertarian view that principles of just acquisition and exchange set limits to the possibility of achieving certain distributive goals. According to Nozick, if the outcome of the application of the principles of just acquisition and exchange is severe inequalities in distribution, the toleration of such inequalities is the price to be paid for justice. By contrast, Rawls argues for the welfare liberal view that principles of just distribution set limits on the possibilities for acquisition and exchange. According to Rawls, if the outcome of the application of the principles of just distribution interferes with previous acquisition and exchange, the toleration of such interference is the price to be paid for justice.

Now for over a decade, this Nozick-Rawls debate has engaged defenders on both sides, and certainly the debate has been characterized by radical disagreement and interminable arguments. But MacIntyre further claims that the debate proceeds from incommensurable premises. According to Macintyre, Rawls' view is ultimately based on the principle that people should be able to keep what they legitimately acquire or earn, and these two principles, MacIntyre contends, cannot be rationally weighed against each other, and, hence, are incommensurable.[20]

MacIntyre claims that this sad state of affairs in which contemporary moral philosophy finds itself has it origin in the Enlightenment of the 17th and the 18th Centuries. As MacIntyre tells the story, key philosophers of that period, such as David Hume and Immanuel Kant, attempted to provide a rational justification for morality while rejecting Aristotelian moral theory. These philosophers began with a conception of human nature as it is and attempted to derive therefrom a justification for adhering to everyday moral precepts. They attempted to show that some feature or features of human nature as it is would lead persons to endorse those everyday moral precepts. To ground morality, Hume appealed to human passions and Kant to human reason. Yet MacIntyre argues that these attempts to ground morality not only failed but had to fail because by rejecting an Aristotelian conception of human nature as it should be and appealing only to human nature as it is, these attempts deprived themselves of just what was needed to ground everyday moral precepts. According to MacIntyre, it is the failure of these attempts to justify morality from the Enlightenment to the present that has led to the current predicament in contemporary moral philosophy. The only way out of this predicament, MacIntyre claims, is for contemporary moral philosophy to return to Aristotelian moral theory, the rejection of which has brought contemporary moral philosophy to its current sorry state.

The Defense of the Ideal

Given that a Communitarian Ideal of the Common Good is not a widely endorsed ideal today, communitarians have frequently chosen to defend their ideal by attacking other ideals, and, by and large, they have focused their attacks on a Welfare Liberal Ideal of Contractual Fairness.

One of the most well-known attacks of this sort has been set out by Michael J. Sandel.[21] What Sandel claims is that a welfare liberal ideal is founded upon an inadequate conception of the nature of persons, according to which none of the particular wants, interest or ends that we happen to have at any given time constitute what we are essentially. According to this conception, we are independent of and prior to all such wants, interest or ends. As Sandel points out, this conception of the nature of persons is similar in certain respects to Kant's doctrine of transcendental subjects of experience. Yet contemporary welfare liberals would not be particularly happy with the comparison since they have attempted to give their conception an empirical rather than a transcendental foundation.

Now Sandel claims that what is inadequate about this conception of the nature of persons is that

> we cannot regard ourselves as independent in this way without great cost to those loyalties and convictions whose moral force consists partly in the fact that the living by them is inseparable from understanding ourselves as the particular persons we are as members of this family or community or nation or people, as bearers of this history, as sons and daughters of that revolution, as citizens of this republic. Allegiances such as these are more

> than values I happen to have or aims I "espouse at any given time." They go beyond the obligations I voluntarily incur and the "natural duties" I owe to human beings as such. They allow that to some I owe more than justice requires or even permits, not by reason of agreements I have made but instead in virtue of those more or less enduring attachments and commitments which taken together partly define the person I am.[22]

Thus, according to Sandel, the conception of the nature of persons required by a welfare liberal ideal is inadequate because it fails to take into account the fact that some of our wants, interests and ends are at least in part constitutive of what we are essentially. Without these desires, interests and ends, we would not be the same persons we presently happen to be.

Sandel contends that welfare liberals are led to rely upon this inadequate conception of persons for reasons that are fundamental to the ideal they want to defend. Specifically, welfare liberals want to maintain the priority of justice and more generally the priority of the right over the good. For example, according to Rawls,

> The principles of right and so of justice put limits on which satisfactions have value; they impose restrictions on what are reasonable conceptions of one's good. We can express this by saying that in justice as fairness the concept of right is prior to that of the good.[23]

To support these priorities, Sandel argues that welfare liberals are led to endorse this inadequate conception of the nature of persons. For example, Rawls argues:

> It is not our aims that primarily reveal our nature but rather the principles that we would acknowledge to govern the background conditions under which these aims are to be found and the manner in which they are to be pursued. *For the self is prior to the ends which are affirmed by it*; even a dominant end must be chosen from among numerous possibilities. ... We should therefore reverse the relation between the right and the good proposed by teleological doctrines and view the right as prior.[24]

What this passage shows, according to Sandel, is that for welfare liberals, like Rawls, the priority of justice and the priority of the right are grounded in the priority of the self to its ends.

Furthermore, Sandel argues that welfare liberals are also led to rely upon this inadequate conception of the nature of persons because they believe that people's native assets should be regarded as common assets on the grounds that no one deserves her or his particular set of native assets. In order to show, therefore, that regarding native assets as common assets does not violate the Kantian injunction never to treat persons merely as means, Sandel claims that welfare liberals are required to conceive of persons as distinct from their assets so that while their assets may be used simply as a means, they themselves would never be so used.

> But, according to Sandel, the notion that only *my assets* are being used as a means, not *me*, threatens to undermine the plausibility, even the coherence, of the very distinction it invokes. It suggests that ... we can take seriously the distinction between persons only by making metaphysically the distinction between a person and his attributes. But this has the consequence of leaving us with a subject *so* shorn of empirically-identifiable characteristics ... as to resemble after all a Kantian transcendent or disembodied subject.[25]

Yet this is just the result that contemporary defenders of a welfare liberal ideal had hoped to avoid.

Practical Reconciliation

Now if a Communitarian Ideal of the Common Good is to be reconciled with our other two ideals, it is necessary to show 1) that, in contrast to what Alasdair MacIntyre claims, contemporary moral philosophy is not characterized by radical disagreement, interminable arguments and incommunsurable premises, 2) that the communitarian objection to a welfare liberal ideal raised by Michael J. Sandel can be answered and 3) that the communitarian ideal does not impose practical requirements that are significantly different from those that are in fact imposed by a welfare liberal ideal. In what follows I propose to establish each of these claims in turn.

The State of Contemporary Moral Philosophy

According to MacIntyre, the only way to avoid the radical disagreement, interminable arguments and incommensurable premises that characterize contemporary moral philosophy is to adopt a Communitarian Ideal of the Common Good based on an Aristotelian moral theory that has been refurbished in certain respects. First of all, the theory would have to abandon any reliance on a metaphysical biology. Secondly, it would have to characterize the human telos in terms of a quest undertaken within a tradition. Thirdly, it would have to allow for the possibility of tragic moral conflict.

But how would an Aristotelian moral theory that has been refurbished in these ways help us to avoid the radical disagreement, interminable arguments and incommunsurable premises which MacIntyre claims characterize contemporary moral philosophy. MacIntyre says little about the particular practices and the tradition which, according to his theory, are to ground an account of the virtues. But without a specification of these practices and tradition, and virtues that are grounded upon them, how are we to avoid the radical disagreements and interminable arguments which MacIntyre claims characterize contemporary moral philosophy?

MacIntyre does explain how his refurbished Aristotelian moral theory avoids choice between incommensurable premises by continuing to recognize the force of the rival moral goods not chosen.[26] But why is that option not also available to defenders of other contemporary views? Surely libertarians can show some regard for meeting basic needs provided the requirements of just appropriation and exchange have been taken into account. For example, they can recognize the goal of meeting basic needs as a requirement of supererogation.[27] Likewise, welfare liberals can show some regard for previous appropriation and exchange, at least after everyone's basic needs have been met.

Yet the capacity of an ethical theory for recognizing the force of the rival moral goods not chosen does not suffice to show that the theory can avoid choice between incommensurable premises. And it no more suffices in the case of MacIntyre's refurbished Aristotelian moral theory than it does in the case of other contemporary theories--virtually all of which have the same capacity. For two theories can have this capacity even when their premises, because they require radically opposed priorities with respect to particular goods, are incommensurable. For example, this would hold if one theory regarded the goal of meeting basic needs to be fundamentally a requirement of obligation and the other regarded that goal to be fundamentally a requirement of supererogation. Consequently, MacIntyre's proposed solution to avoiding choice between incommensurable premises simply will not work.

What will work, I contend, is the approach I have been following in this paper and elsewhere. For to show that the premises of rival political ideals are not really incommensurable and that radical disagreement and interminable arguments can also be avoided, it should suffice to show that when rival political ideals are correctly interpreted, they can be shown to support the same practical requirements. In this way, I claim, it is possible to show that contemporary moral philosophy need not be characterized by radical disagreement, interminable arguments and incommensurable premises.

Sandel's Objection to Welfare Liberalism

Turning next to Sandel's objection to welfare liberalism, as we have seen, Sandel argues that a welfare liberal ideal is objectionable because it is based upon an inadequate conception of the nature of persons. Now at first glance, Sandel's case against welfare liberalism looks particularly strong. After all, Rawls actually does say that "the self is prior to the ends which are affirmed by it" and this claim seems to be just the inadequate conception of the nature of persons that Sandel contends underlies a welfare liberal ideal. Nor is Rawls' claim made specifically about persons in the original position. So Sandel cannot be dismissed for failing to distinguish between the characterization of persons in the original life, as Rawls seems to suggest in a recent article.[28] Nevertheless, Sandel's case against welfare liberalism presupposes that there is no other plausible interpretation that can be given to Rawls' claim than the metaphysical one that Sandel favors. And unfortunately for Sandel's argument, a more plausible interpretation of Rawls' claim does appear to be available.

According to this interpretation, to say that persons are prior to their ends means simply that they are morally responsible for their ends either because they can or could have changed those ends. Of course, the degree to which people can or could have changed their ends is a matter of considerable debate, but what is clear is that it is the degree to which people can or could have changed their ends that determines the degree to which they are morally responsible for those ends.

Nor does this interpretation deny that certain ends may in fact be constitutive of the persons we are, so that if those ends were to change we would become different persons. Of course, the degree to which we think this happens depends upon our theory of personal identity, and most theories of personal identity do not make continuity of one's fundamental aims a requirement of personal identity. But even if we grant that a change in one's fundamental aims could constitute a change in one's personal identity, the crucial question is whether we can or could have brought about such changes (as opposed to having them just happen to us) because the degree to which we can or could have changed our ends determines the degree to which we are responsible for them.

We can see, therefore, that nothing in the above interpretation of Rawls' claim presupposes a self that is metaphysically prior to its ends. Rather the picture we are given is that of a self that is responsible for its ends insofar as its ends are or were revisable. Such a self may well be constituted by at least some of its ends, but it is only responsible for those ends to the degree to which they are or were revisable. So the sense in which a self is prior to its ends is simply moral: insofar as its ends are or were revisable, a self may be called upon to change them or compensate others for them when they turn out to be morally objectionable. Clearly, this interpretation of Rawls' claim avoids any commitment to the inadequate conception of the nature of persons which Sandel contends underlies a welfare liberal ideal.

However, Sandel contends that welfare liberals, like Rawls, are also driven to endorse an inadequate conception of the nature of persons because they believe that people's native assets should be regarded as common assets. Sandel argues that the only way to show that regarding native assets as common assets does not violate the Kantian injunction never to treat persons merely as a means is for welfare liberals to conceive of persons as distinct from their assets, so that while their assets may be used simply as a means, they themselves would never be so used.

Obviously, to evaluate this objection to welfare liberalism, we must first get clear about the conditions under which the Kantian injunction never to treat people merely as a means would be violated. Only then can we determine whether, as Sandel claims, welfare liberals are required to adopt an inadequate conception of the nature of persons in order to avoid violating this Kantian injunction.

Now according to Robert Nozick who first raised this objection to welfare liberalism, the paradigm case of being simply used is that of an exchange in which one party to the exchange does not freely accept the terms or underlying purposes of the exchange.[29] Nozick distinguishes between cases where the exchange is objectionable because one party judges the compensation provided by the other party to be inadequate (I'm being paid too little for my work), and cases where the exchange is objectionable because one party disapproves of the other party's purpose in carrying out the exchange (I don't want my retirement funds invested in South Africa). Unfortunately, Nozick's characterization of his paradigm case is defective, and for reasons Nozick himself should have recognized.

First of all, exchanges that people do not freely accept, that is, forced exchanges, do not necessarily involve simply using people. For example, Nozick allows that in the absence of free agreement a dominant protection agency may be justified in prohibiting independents from employing certain risky procedures provided that adequate compensation is paid by the agency to those independents.[30] And surely Nozick would not want to grant that this is a case of simply using someone. So there can be cases of forced exchanges that do not involve simply using people, even when the force is not being employed in response to any wrongful action.

Secondly, even when people freely accept the terms and purposes of an exchange, this does not preclude their being simply used. People may freely accept the terms and purposes of an exchange only because they have been socially conditioned, against their most fundamental interests, to do so. Nancy Davis, who has pressed this particular objection against Nozick's account, provides the following example:

> The Victim is a lonely, shy and insecure individual, while the Controller is a charismatic charmer. The Controller pays a lot of flattering attention to the Victim with the aim of getting her to become a live-in, all-purpose drudge: what he wants is someone who will attend to his domestic chores, fawn on him, and--since this is what she will be convinced that she wants to

> do--make no fuss about it. Even if the Victim is told that this is what the Controller wants, understands that this is really all that he wants, and agrees to take on the job of all-purpose drudge, we may still think that she is being used. Though she is not ignorant of the Controller's aims and purposes, she is (given her psychological makeup) overwhelmed by his attentions. He is thus able to exercise a strong or special influence over her.[31]

This example seems to be a clear case of where a person is being used even though, in her present circumstances, she has freely agreed to be so used.

So it would seem that the defining characteristics of Nozick's paradigm case of being simply used are neither necessary nor sufficient for an adequate account of that notion. People can be used even when they have freely agreed to the terms and purposes of an exchange or relationship (as in Davis's example) and people may not be used even when they are forced to agree to the terms or purposes of an exchange or relationship (as in Nozick's own example).

What is needed, therefore, to correctly characterize the conditions under which people are being simply used is some suitably idealized standpoint that is relevantly different from the one that the party happens to be in at the moment. Not surprisingly, Rawls claims that his original position can provide us with just such a standpoint.[32] According to Rawls, to avoid simply using people we need only treat them in accord with the requirements that would be chosen in the original position. For example, since a right to welfare would be chosen in the original position, to forcefully require people to help guarantee such a right would not violate the Kantian injunction not to treat people simply as a means. And because such a right would be chosen in the original position, the rich would be violating that injunction in their dealings with the poor, even if the poor had freely agreed to inadequate wages as the only terms of their continued employment by the rich. Alternatively, to appease those who might find this use of Rawls' original position question-begging, we could adopt the idealized standpoint of the "ought" implies "can" principle and avoid simply using people by treating them in accord with the requirements it would be reasonable to ask everyone affected to accept.

Using either standard, it would turn out, that requiring people to use their native assets to help guarantee a right to welfare and a right to equal opportunity would not violate the Kantian injunction not to treat people simply as a means. In view of these interpretations of the Kantian injunction, therefore, there is no need to regard the self as distinct from its assets in order to avoid violating that injunction while recognizing that people are required to regard their native assets as common assets, at least insofar as people are required to use those assets to make a fair contribution toward guaranteeing a right to welfare and a right to equal opportunity. For these reasons, Sandel has failed to show that a welfare liberal ideal is based on an inadequate conception of the nature of persons.

The Practical Requirements of a Communitarian Ideal

Now despite the failure of Sandel's objection to a welfare liberal ideal, there still may be significant practical differences between the requirements of a communitarian and a welfare liberal ideal. MacIntyre has argued that a communitarian ideal, reflecting a fuller conception of the good, would support a much wider range of practical requirements than a welfare liberal ideal. We need to consider, therefore, whether the practical requirements of a communitarian ideal do diverge from the requirements of our other two ideals in this respect.

No doubt there is clearly a difference in aspiration between communitarians and welfare liberals. Communitarians hope to establish a relatively complete conception of the good. By contrast, welfare liberals are doubtful whether any such conceptions can be adequately grounded. Hence, while communitarians are generally inclined to accept the practical requirements defended by welfare liberals, they contend that these requirements are incomplete, since, for example, they neither provide an account of self-regarding virtues nor an account of the requirements of supererogation.

Obviously, there is no contesting the fact that the requirements of welfare liberal ideal, so far elaborated, represent an incomplete moral ideal. yet there does not seem to be any reason why this ideal could not in time be further elaborated to provide a relatively complete moral ideal, particularly given that choice in the original position can take into account all the morally relevant facts about human nature. Indeed, the only knowledge about human nature that is not taken into account in fashioning a welfare liberal ideal is the knowledge of which particular interests happen to be one's own, and from a welfare liberal perspective that knowledge is morally suspect and should be discounted. Thus while it is true that welfare liberals have generally directed their energies at defending basic human rights, there appears to be no reasons why their ideal could not be expanded to include a relatively complete moral ideal.[33]

At the same time, it should be noted that communitarians have done little to remedy this deficiency in welfare liberalism. For example, the conception of the good so far specified and defended by MacIntyre is actually relatively formal when compared with the conceptions developed by rival welfare liberal and libertarian theorists. In fact, communitarians, in general, have yet to provide an adequate defense of even those practical requirements they endorse in common with welfare liberals, let alone provide an adequate defense of additional practical requirements.

It would seem, therefore, that once the requirements of a communitarian ideal are sufficiently elaborated and qualified to meet various objections that can be raised against them, there should be no difficulty reconciling them with the requirements of our other two ideals.[34] At least this is the case with the account of a communitarian ideal that has been so far elaborated by contemporary defenders.

What I have argued, therefore, is that a Welfare Liberal Ideal of Contractual Fairness, a Libertarian Ideal of Liberty, and a Communitarian Ideal of the Common Good, when correctly interpreted, all can be shown to support a right to welfare and a right to equal opportunity. Since these rights are not guaranteed by the U.S. Constitution, I claim that the Constitution, when judged from a moral standpoint, is a fundamentally defective document on this account.

Now it might be objected that this criticism of the U.S. Constitution is inappropriate because it attempts to evaluate the Constitution which for the most part was written two hundred years ago by appealing to contemporary moral and political ideals. But this is to miss the point of my criticism of the Constitution. My criticism is not so much directed at the Constitution as originally written as it is directed at the Constitution as presently amended and interpreted. For whenever a society's constitution can be seen to be morally defective in the light of its acknowledged ideals, it is incumbent upon the members of that society to amend, or at least reinterpret, their constitution to make up for its deficiencies. If I am right, therefore, that when a welfare liberal, libertarian and communitarian ideals are correctly interpreted they all require a right to welfare and a right to equal opportunity, then the U.S. Constitution will remain a fundamentally defective document until it too requires these rights.

Now it might also be objected that greater injustice would be done if we assigned the responsibility for guaranteeing rights to welfare and equal opportunity to the courts rather than to the legislature.[35] But this way of characterizing the alternatives fails to capture the alternative I would favor. For it is certainly possible for the U.S. Constitution to contain rights to welfare and equal opportunity such that the legislature would have the primary task of implementing those rights and the courts only a secondary task of reviewing that implementation, generally improving upon it only in minor respects. This model for constitutional guarantees can be found, for example, in my own state of Indiana and I assume elsewhere. In Indiana, the state constitution guarantees a right to free education and the Indiana legislature has the primary task of implementing that right; the state courts only have a secondary task of reviewing that implementation.

Of course, I have been primarily concerned to argue that rights to welfare and equal opportunity are the fundamental requirements of the moral and political ideals we endorse. This is because the realization that such rights do follow from the ideals we endorse must be widespread in our society before we can realistically face the possibility of implementing such rights at the constitutional level. Nevertheless, even when there is widespread recognition that these rights do follow from our ideals, I would still see their implementation as occurring primarily through legislation and only secondarily through judicial decisions.

NOTES

1. The full argument is to be found in *How to Make People Just* (forthcoming). Parts of the argument have appeared a "A Marxist Critique of Social Contract Theory," *American Philosophical Quarterly* (1982); "A Libertarian Justification for a Welfare State," *Social Theory and Practice* (1985); "The Poor Against the Rich: The Case for Action Welfare Rights," in *Ethics and International Relations*, edited by Anthony Ellis (Manchester: University of Manchester Press, 1986); and "Recent Work on Alternative Conceptions of Justice," *American Philosophical Quarterly* (1986).

2. Each of these approaches faces certain difficulties. The principal difficulty with the first approach is that unless one arbitrarily restricts what is to count as an interference, conflicting liberties will abound, particularly in all areas of social life. The principal difficulty with the second approach is that as long as a person's rights have not been violated, her liberty would not have been restricted either, even if she were kept in prison for the rest of her days. Now I don't propose to try to decide between these two approaches. Later in this section, I argue that on either approach the libertarian ideal can be practically reconciled with a welfare liberal ideal.

3. Isaiah Berlin, *Four Essays on Liberty*. (New York, 1969), pp. XXXVIII-XL.

4. On this point, see Maurice Cranston, *Freedom*. (New York, 1953), pp. 52-53; C.B. Macpherson, *Democratic Theory*. (Oxford, 1973), pp. 95 ff; Joel Feinburg, *Rights, Justice and the Bounds of Liberty*. (Princeton, 1980), Chapter 1.

5. John Hospers, *Libertarianism*. (Los Angeles, 1971), Chapter 7.

6. Alvin Goodman, *A Theory of Human Action*. (Englewood Cliffs, 1970), pp. 208-215; William Frankena, "Obligation and Ability," in *Philosophical Analysis*, edited by Max Black (Ithaca, 1950), pp. 157-175.

Judging from some recent discussions of moral dilemmas by Bernard Williams and Ruth Marcus, one might think that the "ought" implies "can" principle would only be useful for illustrating moral conflicts rather than resolving them. (See Bernard Williams, *Problem of the Self*. (1977), Chapters 11 and 12; Ruth Marcus, "Moral Dilemmas and Consistency," *The Journal of Philosophy* (1980), pp. 121-126. See also Terrance C. McConnell, "Moral Dilemmas and Consistency in Ethics," *Canadian Journal of Philosophy* (1978), pp. 269-287.) But this is true only if one interprets the "can" in the principle to exclude only "what a person lacks the power to do." If one interprets the "can" to exclude in addition "what would involve so great a sacrifice that it would be unreasonable to ask the person to do it," then the principle can be used to resolve moral conflicts as well as state them. Nor could libertarians object to this broader interpretation of the "ought" implies "can" principle since they do not ground their claim to liberty on the existence of irresolvable moral conflicts.

7. See my paper, "Is There a Rationale for Punishment?" *The American Journal of Jurisprudence* (1984).

8. For the argument, see "The Welfare Rights of Distant Peoples and Future Generations: Moral Side-Constraints on Social Policy," *Social Theory and Practice*(1981).

9. Alasdair MacIntyre, *After Virtue* (1st edition). (Notre Dame: University of Notre Dame Press, 1981), p. 152.

10. Ibid., p. 175.

11. Ibid.

12. Ibid., p. 178.

13. Ibid., pp. 187 ff.

14. Ibid., pp. 188-204.

15. Ibid., pp. 133-4, 167-8.

16. Ibid.

17. Ibid., p. 208.

18. Ibid., p. 241.

19. Ibid., Chapter 7.

20. Ibid., 229-231.

21. Michael J. Sandel, *Liberalism and the Limits of Justice* (Cambridge: Cambridge University Press, 1982).

22. Ibid., p. 179.

23. John Rawls, *Theory of Justice*. (Cambridge: Harvard University Press, 1971), p. 31.

24. Rawls, p. 560.

25. Sandel, p. 79.

26. *After Virtue*, p. 208.

27. Of course, I have argued above that libertarians are required to endorse much more.

28. John Rawls, "Justice as Fairness: Political not Metaphysical," *Philosophy and Public Affairs* (1985), pp. 238-9.

29. Robert Nozick, *Anarchy, State and Utopia*. (New York: Basic Books, 1974), pp. 30-32. See also pp. 228-9.

30. Ibid., Chapter 5. This aspect of Nozick's view was also discussed in Chapter 2.

31. Nancy Davis, "Using Persons and Common Sense," *Ethics* 94 (1984), p. 394.

32. Rawls, *A Theory of Justice*, pp. 179-183.

33. Of course, agreement in the original position with respect to a fuller moral ideal presupposes that there is reasonable grounds for greater agreement in society concerning a conception of the good, or at least reasonable grounds for greater agreement concerning the practical requirements of alternative conceptions of the good. But given that I have shown that there is reasonable grounds for practical reconcilation with respect to opposing political ideals, why shouldn't something similar obtain with respect to conceptions of the good?

34. For further argument, see my article, "Recent Work on Alternative Conceptions of Justice," pp. 17-18.

35. I owe this objection to Robert L. Simon.

COMMENT ON JAMES STERBA'S "THE U.S. CONSTITUTION: A FUNDAMENTALLY FLAWED DOCUMENT"

Carlin Romano

Journalists are trained to spot the news in what they cover, and the news in Professor Sterba's paper comes just where it should in a good "newspaper"--in the headline. CONSTITUTION FUNDAMENTALLY FLAWED, it might read in a cheeky tabloid, with a subhead, perhaps, declaring FOUNDING FATHERS SAID TO BLOW IT ON EDUCATION AND WELFARE.

A good editor would be scared to run the story. He'd probably cock an eyebrow and ask the reporter, "Fundamentally flawed?" A document that has survived more than three hundred and fifty official requests to Congress for a new constitutional convention? That has resisted the vast majority of thousands of proposed amendments offered since its ratification? A document that has lasted two hundred years in a world where national constitutions have the life expectancy of a redfish swimming near New Orleans?

But he'd be wrong. Even though the common media equation this year will be that the Constitution's longevity equals its success, that is only one possible standard by which to judge a Constitution. Professor Sterba suggests that the standard is how well the Constitution guarantees rights he claims are required by political ideals we are or ought to be committed to. That too, however, is only one possible standard by which to judge the Constitution. There are others. For instance, how well it accomplishes the aims set by its framers. How well it accomplishes the aims of the people whose government it governs. How well it instantiates the moral and political views of some subset of those people--professional political philosophers, for instance. How well it limits the powers of the government it constitutes.

One apparent fact about deciding whether the Constitution is fundamentally flawed is that the decision depends on what one takes to be the aim of our Constitution. And one needs to be careful in using the word, "fundamental." In his paper, Professor Sterba first writes of the Constitution that "its fundamental weakness is that it fails to guarantee rights to equal opportunity and welfare." He then writes that this failure renders the Constitution "a fundamentally flawed document."

The first claim says only that among the Constitution's weaknesses, failure to guarantee these rights is fundamental. The second claim says that because of this failure, the Constitution as a whole, when its strengths and weaknesses are weighed together, is more weak than strong.

The inference plainly doesn't carry. The largest of many small holes may not sink a very big ship.

While Professor Sterba's paper touches only briefly--two cases--on the actual jurisprudence of the Constitution, and on the relation between it and the derived political rights he claims to establish, his paper seems to me a case of building many access roads to a bridge without building the bridge itself. Anyone who reads or teaches political philosophy knows that it is a fairly easy thing--indeed, the juice on which the discipline runs--to assume certain axioms, derive certain corollaries, sprinkle a fair number of phrases like "it would clearly be unreasonable," or "by any neutral assessment," and make a claim for universality.

So, with certain definitions accepted, and certain "clearlys," "surelys," and "in facts," signed on to, it may be that one can derive rights to equal opportunity and education from a Libertarian Ideal of Liberty and a Communitarian Ideal of the Common Good. It is often possible to get others to accept particular inferences, especially in a seminar. It is much harder to get them to buy the whole package, especially in real life.

The crucial question for Professor Sterba, it seems to me, if he genuinely wishes to tie his project in political philosophy to a claim that the Constitution is fundamentally flawed on his own criterion of Constitutional success, is why the Constitution should embody the particular rights he mentions. Let me point out some difficulties I think he'd encounter here.

1) Sterba argues that if certain rights "follow from a wide range of opposing contemporary moral and political ideals," these rights "would have to be guaranteed by any constitution that claims to be morally defensible."

Does this follow? Although there is no room to go into the issue, it should be noted that the degree to which a legal system--let alone a constitution--must instantiate a community's morality, remains controversial, and there will be H.L.A. Harts arguing with Lon Fullers, I suspect, for many generations to come. Clearly, this does not follow automatically, and Sterba needs to address the issues of this debate.

It can also be asked why, in order to be morally defensible, a constitution must guarantee such rights rather than simply permit them, or provide them. Recall that Article I, section 8, does not say that Congress shall have the duty, or the obligation, to provide for the general welfare of the United States. It says "The Congress shall have the power . . . to . . . provide . . . for the general welfare of the United States. . . ." Recall also that, Charles McIlwaine pointed out in his short book, *Constitutionalism Ancient and Modern*, "constitutionalism has one essential quality: it is a legal limitation on government." In regard to actual entitlements, our constitution primarily sets out what a government can do and must not do--not what it must do, except in regard to bureaucratic procedure.

Consider an example. Suppose our constitution included an Article stating that all rights otherwise granted in the Constitution can be eliminated by a vote of ninety percent of the state legislatures. Suppose also that the Article had never been acted upon, and, in fact, was widely viewed the way many extant state laws on fornication are viewed--as an odd curiosity. Suppose, thirdly, that this constitution not only provides the rights our current one does, but also lavish rights to equal opportunity and education.

Would this Constitution be fatally flawed on Sterba's view? I put that out as a question.

2) Sterba's requirement that the Constitution guarantee certain rights as a condition of being *not* fundamentally flawed, also does not sit well with his statement, late in his paper, that his criticism "is not so much directed at the Constitution as originally written as it is directed at the Constitution as presently amended and interpreted."

I take it that the "presently" in that sentence does not communicate its main meaning, "soon to happen," but "currently." If one accepts, as Sterba seems to in his later remark, that the Constitution comprises both the document and its subsequent jurisprudence, one can hardly ask at the same time for guarantees. It is, after all, an established rule of Supreme Court jurisprudence that the Court can overrule itself. That is the extreme case, but in softer fashion, the court is trimming and expanding rights all the time. If the Court can only escape the predicament of being fundamentally flawed by guaranteeing exactly the static amount of education and equal opportunity that Sterba might wish, he has set a very high standard for the Constitution to meet. I would think that if Sterba wants to stick to the evolving Constitution as his target, he should drop the word "guarantee" and replace it with something like "provide."

3) Sterba assumes that the Constitution does not provide rights to education and equal opportunity on the basis of two decisions, despite his recognition of the evolutionary nature of the Constitution. This ignores the fact that implicit in the notion of constitutional interpretation that accepts an evolving model of the Constitution is the idea that a right always existed in the Constitution even if only detected at a stage subsequent to its ratification. So, for instance, someone who accepts today that the Constitution includes a right to privacy does not say, "the Constitution has included a right to privacy since X vs. Y," or something like that, but "the Constitution includes a right to privacy."

Thus, if Sterba does take the evolving Constitution as his model, it does not seem he can flatly assert that it is fundamentally flawed in the ordinary meaning of "fundamentally." I would submit that a Constitution capable of satisfying Sterba's concrete distributive wishes with a mere shift in membership on the court, or even significant dicta by a justice in a majority opinion, is something less than fundamentally flawed.

4) This leads to a related hesitation about what is needed, other than political will, to "deflaw" the Constitution on Sterba's standards. Constitutional rights in the U.S. law have come through interpretations of the commerce clause or equal protection clause. Indeed, it has been said that post-New Deal jurisprudence in regard to the commerce clause "left no significant limits on what Congress could regulate, with a little skillful drafting, via the commerce power." The courts even flirted, during the Warren era, with the idea of a right to welfare, most notably in William Douglas' opinions on the economic implications of equal protection. As a result, the extreme elasticity of the commerce clause also undermines Sterba's view that the current Constitution flatly rejects rights to education or equal opportunity.

5) A fifth reservation in regard to Sterba's "news" about the Constitution relates to his apparent certainty, implicit at various points in his paper, about the reasonableness of wanting these rights instantiated in the U.S. Constitution. In the society I see and read about every day, opinion continues to differ sharply about the proper degree to which people should be entitled to welfare and educational benefits from the federal government, and under what conditions. And opinions have differed for a long time. Locke's own notion of charity included restrictions on the mobility of unemployed persons, the assignment of children to government workhouses, and free provision of subsistence food and housing only to those wholly incapable of work. Through most of the nineteenth century, in the United States, welfare was widely seen to be a local and state responsibility, not a federal one. Sterba's paper suggests that in the absence of constitutional guarantees to certain rights, people face certain suffering. It does not take into account the role of state and local governments, and how their actions and responsibilities affect a judgment on the adequacy of the Federal constitution.

The differing opinions have been articulated not just in the courts, but on the Presidential level. In 1859, when Congress passed Dorothea Dix's bill granting federal land to states for mental hospitals, President Franklin Pierce vetoed it, saying the Constitution gave no authority "for making the Federal Government the great almoner of public charity throughout the United States." We know that around the turn of the century, as Congress began to use the commerce clause power to pass progressive legislation, that the Supreme Court rejected federal social welfare intervention for decades before it switched its tune under the pressure of the New Deal. So, we heard from Roosevelt in 1932 that the federal government had "a continuing responsibility for the broader public welfare." And the Court, in the 1937-38 term, finally responded.

Yet even then, Pierce's statement continued to be cited in dissent. And, as Roger Smith observes in his book, *Liberalism and American Constitutional Law*, "the government's new role was generally understood to represent nothing more than a current legislative choice of the majority. Hence, it officially rested on new judgments of expedient policy for the general welfare and not on new claims of unqualified fundamental or constitutional rights . ... The Social Security Program was misleadingly portrayed as a self-supporting insurance scheme rather than as a welfare program. ... Instead of endeavoring to give Social Security benefits the status of a constitutional right, Roosevelt insisted on a payroll tax as the official funding device ... ." And the laissez faire view still exists among conservatives that poverty is a personal responsibility, and that public aid can be self-defeating by creating a permanent lower class.

We can add to this historical lack, in the U.S., of the domestic consensus on federal obligations in regard to welfare, the point made by two political scientists in a new book entitled *The Welfare State: East and West*, that assumptions about welfare differ sharply today on the international level, even among such sophisticated countries as Sweden, the U.S., Japan, West Germany, Israel and France. Since a constitution by its nature, demands consensus judgments, and since Sterba's arguments for guaranteed rights rather than provided rights seems weak, why should decisions on such rights, in the clear absence of consensus, be elevated from a legislative to a constitutional level?

6) A last query. Does it make sense to speak of a generalized "right to welfare," and a generalized "right of equal opportunity"? In the real world of

politics, there is only a right to a certain amount of welfare, to certain kinds of opportunity. It can be argued, for instance, that the Constitution grants us equal opportunity to express ourselves under the First Amendment, or to plead the Fifth Amendment. It is also clear, thanks to the First Amendment, that we have an equal opportunity to educate ourselves by reading, and perhaps availing ourselves of public libraries.

On that argument, Sterba's claim that the Constitution does not offer these rights is not strictly true. What is does not offer is a more specific form of these rights--taking Sterba's court cases, a right to a certain amount of money spent in one's school district, or a certain amount of monthly money in one's mailbox. If these are in fact the entitlements not guaranteed, their absence seems less capable of rendering the Constitution fundamentally flawed.

THE DANGERS OF CONSTITUTIONOLATRY

Sterba's Disturbing View of the Role of Constitutional Rights

A Commentary

Robert C. L. Moffat

James Sterba sets out his theses boldly in the first two sentences of his Paper: "The fundamental strength of the U.S. Constitution is that it guarantees rights to religious and political liberty. Its fundamental weakness is that it fails to guarantee rights to equal opportunity and welfare." (Sterba, p. 1) Those theses provide us examples of four different sorts of idolatry of the Constitution.

First, it is a modern conceit to claim that the strength of the Constitution is the protection of *any* right. Sterba's claim represents a greatly different set of priorities from those pursued by the framers. It is easy to forget that the Bill of Rights applied only to the Federal government for almost a century after the adoption of the Constitution. The reason for its addition to the Constitution in the first place was the fear of the abuse of power centralized in the national government. That fear had already generated, not only a well-defined separation of powers, but also an elaborate system of checks and balances in the original document. That limitation of power was for the framers the genius of the charter. Thoughtful persons might consider the strength of our Constitution to be its success thus far in maintaining social order despite limits that are far more severe than those imposed on any other major government.

Second, the most fundamental right protected by the Constitution is not the protection of religious and political liberty, but the guarantee of due process of law. Without that assurance, all the rest of the protections become so much surplusage, because they are legally meaningless. A constitution may guarantee your religious liberty and your right to vote and speak freely, but that guarantee provides you with no independent judicial protection of the liberty unless you are entitled to due process.[1] Without judicial enforcement, your liberties are mere "paper" rights with no more meaning than whatever sham procedures the government of the moment happens to employ to "enforce" them. Jeremy Bentham, it is true, might intervene on the ground that the government would still be limited by "the habit of obedience."[2] But, if you belong to a minority group to whom the majority is not sympathetic, the constraint on the government provided by public opinion will be of little consolation.

Third, all rights need be neither constitutional nor judicially-enforced. Sterba's assumption that guaranteed rights necessarily mean judicially-enforced constitutional rights depends on the proposition that no other form of right is worth either considering or holding. But many constitutional rights are not enforced by the courts. One example is the guarantee of a republican form of government. Is it worthless because its enforcement depends on the legislative branch? Some constitutional guarantees are not enforced by any branch. Indeed, many important rights are not mentioned in the Constitution, because the framers fashioned that document to provide a structure of government and not a declaration of abstract ideals.

As a practical matter, judicial action is limited by the fact that only some rights are appropriate for judicial enforcement. Generally, unpopular minorities will have the greatest need for judicial protection. Even then, judicial action will usually be feasible only when the relief to be granted consists of restraining action rather than commanding it. This again is a point that Bentham touched on, distinguishing such negative power from the positive power wielded by legislatures. He thought that proposals such as the

American constitutional experiment to clothe the judiciary with negative power would not succeed in transferring "the supreme authority from the legislative to the judicial."[3] Only positive power would suffice for Bentham. The framers, on the other hand, deliberately sought negative power for the judiciary.

Sterba's proposed rights to welfare and equal opportunity appear to require the exercise, not of negative power, but of positive (legislative) power. But there are reasons why we should doubt the wisdom of having the courts wield such positive power. Legislation requires the combination of ideals and enforcement. The problem of enforcement, however, involves fundamental difficulties such as establishing adequate standards to determine the meaning of the right and finding appropriate means for enforcing it. For example, equality of opportunity is an ideal to which the court would consider itself committed as one aspect of the equal protection clause. But a statement of such general sweep must be given meaning in concrete cases. Then the Court must ask whether it is possible to develop firm standards for application in that particular area and whether there are practicable means of enforcement.

Upon examination, Sterba's criticism of the decisions in the school finance and welfare search cases are excellent examples of the call for the exercise by the Court of what turn out to be Bentham's positive powers. The Court held back from decisions favoring the plaintiffs in those cases at least partly because such decisions would have required significant degrees of judicial legislation in order to effectuate the decrees. Formulas to attain equality in school district financing would reasonably have to have been expected to be even more complicated than those employed in the reapportionment cases. Obviously, slogans such as "one child, one dollar" would not provide such guidance to the lower courts. Moreover, the details of implementation promised to be vastly more complex even than the tangles generated by the reapportionment cases.[4]

Similarly, an affirmative decision in the welfare search case announcing a "right" to welfare would commit the Court to determine in future cases just how *much* welfare one may claim as a matter of right. Even supposing that legal standards were available upon which to found such a determination, the Court would still be stuck with the age-old problem of figuring out how to enforce its decrees. In a very few desegregation decisions, federal district courts went to the unprecedented length of taking a school district into receivership, managing it for a limited time, and even levying and collecting taxes. With the advent of judicially-enforced welfare rights, the courts could venture into the really interesting political thicket of taking the United States Congress into receivership and directing the expenditure of federal funds so as to satisfy their decrees. That would be an employment of sufficient positive power to persuade even a Bentham that the Court was truly the sovereign (at least until after the revolution). Perhaps, it is just this sort of judicial foolhardiness that inspired Lon Fuller to imagine a "War of the Judges" in one of his hypothetical future jurisdictions.[5]

Fourth, there is no need to include every social ideal in the Constitution, whether or not judicial enforcement is sought. Sterba complains that ours is flawed because of its failure to embrace all of the society's "acknowledged ideals." (Sterba, p. 18) In order to remedy that fault, Sterba might opt for the inclusion of all societal ideals as is done in many Continental constitutions. But the significance from our perspective is that those constitutions are not documents whose primary function is legal. In such legal systems, the fundamental law is provided by the Code. In contrast, the primary functions of our Constitution are to constitute the government and to set out the rules of government which are to be enforced by the courts. The great English constitutional scholar A. V. Dicey noted that the Continental practices with disdain, because in his view superior protection was provided by a legal remedy rather than any mere "ideal" right.[6] Consequently, Dicey saw the English unwritten Constitution as superior to the declarations of individual rights in Continental constitutions where judicial power to protect such rights did not exist.

In fact, Dicey saw that the "inflexibility of the constitution tempts legislators to place among constitutional articles maxims which (though not in their nature constitutional) have special claims upon respect and observance."[7] Quite accurately, Dicey noted that such non-constitutional matters given the stature of supreme law may often be trivial, and, almost in the same breath, implied his contempt for such " 'guaranteed' rights," considering them to be nothing more than "principles or petty rules which are supposed to have a claim of legal sanctity."[8] The real worry raised by such foolishness is that the legal purposes of the Constitution will be confused by littering the document with momentary fads. Now classic examples of such proposals are the Lawyers Guild proposal in the late thirties to put the Wagner Labor Act into the Constitution or the amendment proposed by the American Bar Association in the fifties to limit income taxes to 25%.[9]

Sterba might, nonetheless, call for a statement of ideals in the constitutional document that would involve no implications of judicial enforcement. Notably, Dicey disapproved of cluttering the document with such non-essentials, even though he thought that such posturing was without legal significance. However, in this respect, Dicey's understanding of our Constitution was inadequate, because he underestimated the importance of judicial review as an omnipresent, potent weapon of enforcement. That factor of uncertainty would require special precautions in order to make possible the inclusion in the Constitution of mere ideals. One possible solution would borrow from the practice of our political parties of writing "platforms." Similarly, we could include in our Constitution a separate section clearly labeled "Ideals" and clearly marked "Not to be enforced by the courts." Moreover, in order to keep the statement of ideals current, we could call for a national convention every ten or twenty years to revise and update it. That way we would not have to worry whether rights to welfare and equally funded schools will turn out to be of enduring import. Even if they represent the momentary zenith of liberal ideals, that would be taken care of by the next "Ideal" convention. That seems an appropriate way to address symbolic measures. We must simply take care not to confuse such matters with issues of constitutional law.

On the other hand, if Sterba decides he wants judicial enforcement of his rights, no matter now much positive power might be required to enforce them, Dicey's analysis poses one more obstacle to thwart his desires. What really matters, Dicey argues, is not what is written down, but what the tradition of the courts is with respect to those provisions. No matter how much we may clutter the document with every conceit of the moment, what really counts is judicial philosophy. Many provisions have been ignored even by the most activist courts; the privileges and immunities clause of the 14th Amendment is just one example.[10] Even when our most activist courts have undertaken their boldest rampages into constitutional "interpretation," Dicey's ghost still remains to admonish us that the "magic" is in the interpretative philosophy and not in the provision interpreted.

Let us suppose, however, that Sterba is successful in converting the Court to a judicial philosophy that carries it on to all of the bold, positive steps necessary to implement his rights, for it is clear that a vigorous liberal activism would be required to make them judicially effective. Admittedly, even Bentham would have to be impressed by such massive positive power. But where is the answer to the framer's question: If the courts are exercising positive (legislative) power, what branch remains to exercise negative (judicial) power in order to restrain the abuse of positive judicial power by reviewing the judiciary's legislation? That question poses no embarrassment and requires no answer if one lacks conviction that the genius of the framers is reflected in their grasp of the importance of negative power. If, however, proponents of "liberal" activism such as Sterba are inclined to ignore that question, they may soon face a true test of their disdain for negative power: the deployment of positive power by "conservative" judicial activists. (Indeed, the bold move Sterba would have the Court make from the legal into the political sphere would likely increase the chance that his "gains" might in turn be swept away in a conservative countertide.) If he can accept that prospect with equanimity, he must win our admiration for consistent adherence to his philosophy of the Constitution. Even so, I confess my preference for the much more modest vision of the framers.

In the revised version of his paper, Sterba attempts to equivocate on this pivotal issue of enforcement. He would like "the U.S. Constitution [to] contain rights to welfare and equal opportunity such that the legislature would have the primary task of implementing those rights and the courts only a secondary task of reviewing that implementation, generally improving upon it only in minor respects." (Sterba, p. 31) The most sensible interpretation of this proposal would call for the addition to the Constitution of specific Congressional powers to provide welfare and equal opportunity. That step, however, would not satisfy Sterba for two reasons. First, constitutional rights to welfare and equality would not thereby be created. Second, judicial enforcement or supervision of those rights would not be established. Despite Sterba's attempt to have it both ways, he cannot escape the necessity of choice. If Sterba's Court did not exercise final authority, its opinions would merely advisory, a practice long held not to be encompassed within the judicial power under Article III of our Constitution. Moreover, Sterba's rights would be backed by no guarantee of independent enforcement. On the other hand, if the Court were to have the final say, it would encounter all the problems of standards, implementation, and potential conflict with the legislative branch that I have discussed above.

NOTES

1. See Moffat, *Legality or Legalism? Some Critical Reflections on the Quest for Due Process*, 39 U. Fla. L. Rev. 555-81 (1987).

2. J. Bentham, *Fragment of Government and Principles of Morals and Legislation* 99 (ch. 4, Sec. 36) (Harrison ed. 1948). On the "Habit of Obedience," see Moffat, *Bentham and Hart on Constitutional Limitations: Some Bicentennial Reflections*, 3 (4) Int'l J. Applied Philosophy 51, 57 (Fall 1987).

3. *Id*. at 98 (ch. 4, Sec. 33).

4. Fuller, "The Case of the Contract Signed on Book Day," in *The Problems of Jurisprudence* 71, 73 (temp. ed. 1949).

5. See L. Fuller, *The Morality of Law* 178 (rev. ed. 1969).

6. A. V. Dicey, *Law of the Constitution* 198 (9th ed. 1948); see also id. at 200.

7. *Id*. at 153.

8. *Id*. at 154.

9. Those examples are offered by Lon Fuller in the process of observing that "we should resist the temptation to clutter up [our Constitution] with amendments relating to substantive matters." Fuller, *American Legal Philosophy at Mid-Century*, 6 J. Legal Ed. 457, 463-64 (1954).

10. *Slaughter-house Cases*, 83 U.S. (16 Wall.) 36 (1873).

A VIRTUALLY PERFECT DOCUMENT: RIGHTS AND THE U.S. CONSTITUTION

A Commentary

Tibor R. Machan

Is the United States Justly Governed?

The United States of America has had its famous constitution since 1787, yet the document is still a subject of much debate. Socialists and welfare statists criticize it on grounds that it fails to recognize the rights to equal welfare and equal opportunity. Libertarians, in turn, would lament that it fails to give explicit legal support to the separation of state and culture--including education, the arts, medicine, commerce--in short, society and culture--in the firm manner in which it did secure the separation of state and religion.

Yet, undeniably, among all the political systems throughout the globe and the ages, that of the United States of America has come closest--at least to my knowledge--to implementing some crucial features of the libertarian natural rights theory. This is due, in part, to the direct influence of John Locke and Montesquieu, and the indirect influence of Aristotle--via the reading and thinking of the Founding Fathers--on the political philosophy (the Declaration of Independence) and the legal system (the Constitution) of the United States.

Of course, the fundamental legal document of a society cannot be divorced completely from that society's other elements and values. And to the extent that we take religion to include the moral and political values of a culture, the constitution will have to be connected with religion--or philosophy. The U.S. Constitution endorses the separation of state and church only in the respect that the state must not be connected with any *organized* religion, any particular organized agency promulgating some set of convictions. But of course religion and philosophy do carry political impact.

The Founding Fathers were largely deists and fideists and believed that while religion had a vital role in the lives of people, it would be best to confine it to their personal lives. The public domain was to be left to be dealt with in terms of secular concepts that are accessible to anyone and everyone who would just use his or her mind--as Locke put it, consult Reason. The public realm is properly secular because to know about it requires a faculty we all possess and can use as a matter of our own initiative. Revelation--the source of supernatural belief or faith--is not available to just any person. It requires divine selection, grace--assuming it exists at all. Religion, in short, is not a proper subject for discerning and especially for grounding the principles of public life.

The point of keeping at least the federal government out of private and social (religious, economic, parental, artistic, etc.) life is to reduce the power of the state or government, to make it serve very specific, limited goal, not to skirt totalitarianism.

Of course, the terms of such government--the standards--would themselves come from certain convictions, philosophical ideals about justice, order, stability, liberty, equality, etc. The United States' Declaration of Independence is, as already noted, a kind of philosophical foreword to the U.S. Constitution. It aims to provide the national consensus on values that should guide the more detailed Constitutional processes of the society.

In large measure the U.S. Constitution expresses the natural rights libertarian political philosophy of John Locke, although it is more of a political compromise on some divergent values than is the Declaration of Independence. (It is a dubious and at any rate irrelevant charge that the

Lockean / American doctrine expresses an ideology. This is an insulting view and not worth discussion here.)

What is compromised in the U.S. Constitution? Abraham Lincoln knew the answer when he noted that the Constitution did not fully enough implement the philosophy of the Declaration of Independence. Lincoln opposed slavery on the grounds, as he put it, that "no man is good enough to govern another man, without that other's consent."[1] Many who believed in slavery on humanitarian grounds--for example, the famous American socialist George Fitzhugh (in his book *Sociology for the South; or, the Failure of Free Society)*--denied this view, in particular when it came to blacks toward whom they advocated paternalism. They knew, along with Lincoln, that the unalienable rights to life, liberty and the pursuit of happiness are the central feature of the American political tradition. But they disagreed with Lincoln and the libertarian strain in American culture that however noble may be the goal for the sake of which unauthorized governance of one's fellows would be exercised, it is fundamentally wrong.

The initial version of the U.S. Constitution tolerated slavery and this, of course, was its gravest flaw. But some earlier as well as contemporary critics of the U.S. Constitution are suggesting that its fundamental flaw is that it does not include a guarantee of the rights to welfare and equal opportunity, rights that are supposedly implied in the rights that are listed in the Declaration of Independence, the Lockean rights to life, liberty and pursuit of happiness. This guarantee should be extended at least to the more disadvantaged members--just as Fitzhugh believed.

Quite rightly, in my view, no such rights are stated or are desirable in the Declaration. To indicate why, I will examine the argument of one welfare statist critic of the U.S. Constitution, James Sterba. It is Sterba's main contention that *the* crucial flaw of the U.S. Constitution is that it fails to guarantee so called rights to welfare and equal opportunity.

Lacking Welfare Rights

Sterba and others would maintain that the U.S. Constitution and indeed any constitution should guarantee the basic rights of everyone to "receive the goods and resources necessary for preserving" ourselves. But this is not what Locke held human beings have a right to. They have the right, rather, not to be killed, attacked, and deprived of their property--by persons in or outside of government. And the U.S. Constitution thus far seems to have secured these rights with considerable vigilance, although by no means adequately--which is why defending these rights is a constant and continued theoretical and practical task. That indeed seems to have secured the unique fame of the United States of America, guided largely by tenets Sterba considers fundamentally flawed.

Sterba claims that various political outlooks would have to endorse these "rights." He sets out to show, in particular, that welfare rights follow from libertarian theory itself.[2] First let us make clear that Sterba wishes to show that *if* Lockean libertarianism is correct, then we all have rights to welfare and equal (economic, etc.) opportunity. What I wish to show is that since Lockean libertarianism--as developed in this work--is true, and since the rights to welfare and equal opportunity require their violation, no one has these latter rights. The reason some people, including Sterba, believe otherwise is that they have found some very rare instances in which some citizens could find themselves in circumstances that would require disregarding rights altogether. This would be in situations that cannot be characterized to be "where peace is possible."[3] And every major libertarian thinker from John Locke to present has treated these kinds of cases.[4]

Let us be clear again about what Sterba sets out to show. It is that libertarians are philosophically unable to escape the welfare statist implication of their commitment to negative liberty. This means that despite their belief that they are only supporting the enforceable rights of every person not to be coerced by other persons, libertarians must accept, by the logic of their own position, that individuals also possess basic enforceable rights to being provided with various services from others. He holds, then, that basic negative rights imply basic positive rights.

Negative Rights and Welfare "Rights"

To Lockean libertarians the ideal of liberty means that we all, individually, have the right not to be constrained against our consent within our realm of authority--ourselves and our belongings. Sterba states that for such libertarians "Liberty is being unconstrained by persons from doing what one has a right to do."[5] Sterba adds, somewhat misleadingly, that for Lockean libertarians "a right to life [is] a right not to be killed unjustly and a right to property [is] a right to acquire goods and resources either by initial acquisition or voluntary agreement."[6] Sterba does realize that these rights do not entitle one to receive from others the goods and resources necessary for preserving one's life.

A problem with this formulation of the Lockean libertarian view is that political justice--not the justice of Plato, which is best designated in our time as "perfect virtue"--for natural rights theorists presupposes individual rights. One cannot explain rights in terms of justice but must explain justice in terms of rights.

For a Lockean libertarian to possess any basic right to receive the goods and resources necessary for preserving one's life conflicts with possessing the right not to be killed, assaulted, or stolen from. The latter are rights Lockean libertarians consider to be held by all individual human beings. To normally, legally protect and maintain--i.e., enforce--the former right would often require the violation of the latter. A's right to the food she has is incompatible with B's right to take this same food. Not both the rights could be fundamental in an integrated legal system. The situation of one having rights to welfare, etc., and others having rights to life, liberty and property is thus theoretically and practically intolerable. The point of a system of rights is the securement of mutually peaceful and consistent moral conduct on the part of human beings. As Ayn Rand observed, " 'Rights' are . . . the link between the moral code of a man and the legal code of a society, between ethics and politics. *Individual rights are the means of subordinating society to moral law.*"[7]

In this respect all rights theorists agree: basic rights in a legal system serve to secure a moral order in society. But those advocating negative rights hold that this order is best secured when we provide people with reliable, ongoing, flexible but stable borders wherein they can choose their own conduct. And property rights are the concrete implementation of this purpose. Those who advocate positive rights see human beings as somehow naturally in a collective situation, as members of a natural team, owing each member support for some common purpose, even if it reduces the freedom of choice and prospect of success for some individuals.

To bolster his attempt to derive positive rights from (libertarian) negative rights, Sterba asks us--in another discussion of his views--to consider what he calls "a *typical* conflict situation between the rich and the poor." He says that in his situation "the rich, of course, have more than enough resources to satisfy their basic needs. By contrast, the poor lack the resources to meet their most basic needs even though *they have tried all the means available to them that libertarians regard as legitimate for acquiring such resources"* (my emphasis).

Now the objective of a theory of rights noted by Rand would be defeated if rights were typically in conflict. Some bureaucratic group would have to keep applying its moral intuitions on numerous occasions when rights claims would *typically* conflict. A constitution is suited to the kind of beings human beings are--namely, moral agents--if it helps to remove at least the largest proportion of such decisions from the realm of arbitrary (intuitive) choice and avail a society of men and women of objective guidelines that are reasonably integrated, not in relentless discord.

Most critics of libertarianism assume some doctrine of basic needs which they invoke to show that whenever basic needs are not satisfied for some people, while others have "resources" which are not basic needs for them, the former have just claims against the latter. (The language of resources of course loads the argument in the critic's favor since it suggests that these goods simply come into being and happen to be in the possession of some people, quite without rhyme or reason, arbitrarily, as John Rawls claims.[8])

This doctrine is full of difficulties--for example, it lacks any foundation for why the needs of some persons must be claims upon the lives of others? And why are there such needs anyway--to what end are they needs, and whose ends are these and why are not the person or persons whose needs they are held responsible for supplying the needs? (Needs as such lack any decisive force in moral argument without the prior justification of the purposes or goals their satisfaction serves to fulfill. A thief has a basic need of skills and powers that are clearly not justified if theft is morally unjustified. If, however, the justification of basic needs, such as food and other resources, presupposes the value of human life, and if the value of human life justifies, as I would argue, the principle of the natural right of life, liberty and property, then the fulfillment of basic needs for food may not involve the violation of these rights. But some ways of attaining such needs could--including forced redistribution of wealth).

Libertarianism versus 'Out Implies Can'

I will leave these concerns aside for now and attend, instead, to the central criticism Sterba offers of Lockean libertarianism. He claims that without guaranteeing welfare and equal opportunity rights, Lockean libertarianism violates the most basic tenet of any morality, namely, that "ought" implies "can."

The thrust of " 'ought' implies 'can' " is that one ought to do that which one is free to do, i.e., that one is morally responsible only for those acts that one has or has had the power either to choose to engage in or to choose not to engage in. This is not so different from the common sense legal precept that if one is not sound of mind and uncoerced, one cannot be criminally culpable. Only free agents, capable of choosing between right and wrong, are open to moral evaluation. This indeed is the reason that many so called moral theories fail to be anything more than value theories. They omit from consideration the issue of self-determinism. If hard or soft determinism is true, morality is impossible, although values need not disappear.[9]

If Sterba were correct about Lockean libertarianism typically contradicting "ought" implies "can," his argument would be decisive. (There are few arguments against this principle I know of and they have not convinced me.[10]) It is because Karl Marx's and Herbert Spencer's systems typically, normally, indeed in every case violate this principle that they are not bona fide moral systems. And quite a few others may be open to similar charge.[11]

I am not, of course, certain "beyond a shadow of doubt" that libertarianism might not (conceivably, possibly) be flawed in the way Sterba claims. It would be dogmatic, aprioristic, to hold that. No system is so well established that one who agrees with it should regard it impossible that it could be flawed. Political theories can be expected to be proven true only beyond reasonable doubt, and it is reasonable doubt that I find difficult to justify concerning the merits of libertarianism. For the time being I will concentrate on what could be wrong about Sterba's suggestion. I will do this by considering the cases he offers which he considers indicative of the problems he identifies in Lockean libertarianism.

What is or is not Typical

The case Sterba offers in support of the view that Lockean libertarianism violates "ought" implies "can" is, first of all, not a typical one and thus does not unwittingly imply the welfare state. Sterba offers his strongest argument when he observes that "ought" implies "can" is violated "when the rich prevent the poor from taking what they require to satisfy their basic needs . . . though they have tried all the means available to them that libertarians regard as legitimate for acquiring such resources."[11]

Is Sterba right that such are typical cases in a libertarian society? Are the rich and poor, even admitting for the moment that there is some simple division of people into such economic groups, at each others' throats all the time? Even with the homeless people--of whom some may be truly helpless, unfortunate and not either the victims of rights violation or self-neglect--it is clear that many find help without having to resort to theft.

Clearly there can be cases in a system of justice that legally protects and preserves property rights where a rich person could personally (or call in the police to) prevent some poor person from taking what belongs to her--e.g., a chicken that the poor person might use to feed himself. Since subsequent to such prevention the poor person might starve or at least become seriously ill, Sterba asks the rhetorical question, "Have the rich, then, in contributing to this result, killed the poor, or simply let them die; and if they have killed the poor, have they done so unjustly?"[12] His answer is that they have.

Sterba holds that a system that accords with the Lockean libertarian's idea that the rich person's preventive action is just "imposes an unreasonable sacrifice upon" the poor, one "that we could not blame them for trying to evade." Not permitting the poor to act to satisfy their basic needs is to undermine the precept that "ought" implies "can," since, as Sterba claims, that precept means, for the poor, that in all reason they ought to satisfy their basic needs. This they must have the option to do if they ought to do it.

Paternalism as Remedy of Exploitation

Another case that supposedly shows that Lockean libertarianism wrongfully restricts the state to protecting only rights to life, liberty and property is provided by Nancy Davis, concerning the "lonely, shy and insecure individual" who is being taken advantage of, with her consent, by "a charismatic charmer." Here Sterba asserts that "This example seems to be a clear case of where a person is being used even though, in her present circumstances, she has freely agreed to be so used." This case seems to support the thesis that despite the presence of full, informed consent, the terms of interaction between some people is immoral and, presumably, may be prohibited or regulated by the state. This kind of case is supposed to support a version of paternalism,[13] clearly one feature of welfare liberalism. Securing a justification of this practice would certainly assist the anti-libertarian, welfare statist argument. For if we are generally justified in taking care of other adults without permission from them individually, officials of the state would be justified doing so as well.

Libertarianism versus Welfare Statism

When people defend their property, what are they doing? They are responding to the acts of someone who would take from them something unjustly, something to which they and not others have a right. As such these acts of prevention are preserving libertarian justice. They are making it possible for men and women in society to retain their own sphere of jurisdiction intact, protect and preserve their own "moral space."[14] Those who mount the attack, in turn, refuse to act in such a way that what they do does not encroach upon the moral space of their victims.

Now the point that cuts against the above scenario is that on some occasions there can be people who, with no responsibility for their situation, cannot survive without disregarding the rights of others and taking from them what they need. This is indeed possible. But is it typical?

The argument that starts with this assumption about a society is already not comparable to Lockean libertarianism. That system concludes that "peace is possible" and so individual rights, the protection of which free men and women from those who would thwart their efforts at flourishing, are the best legal foundations for a good society. The underlying notion of human nature in such a theory rejects the description of the world implicit in Sterba's picture, whereby people are *typically* in conflict, so that some have and others must take from them in order to survive, with no other alternative available to them. The Lockean libertarian, in short, abates the worries of those rights theorists who would attempt to guarantee rights to service from others by having confidence in the willingness and general circumstances of *virtually all persons* to make headway in life. Once they are free of autocratic rule and tyranny, the rest will be taken care of as best as that can be expected in an uncertain world and amongst beings who are capable of both good and evil.

We have already noted that the idea of "satisfying basic needs" can involve the difficulty of distinguishing between whose actions are properly to be so characterized. Rich persons are indeed satisfying their basic needs with their protection and preservation of their property rights. That the right to private property is a necessary ingredient of a just and decent society cannot be established here but I can say that the idea of a definite, continuing and stable realm of personal jurisdiction in everyone's life, extending over such items as land, minerals, stocks, computer programs, poems, musical arrangements, etc., is indispensable for a full conceptualization of someone's capacity to lead a morally responsible life. This life depends not on some amount of property but on the right to property--to obtain and use valued items. The Lockean libertarian understands that private property rights are morally justified precisely as the concrete requirement for delineating the sphere of jurisdiction of each person's moral authority, where her own judgment is decisive.[15] Once this basis for the right to property is recognized, and the argument is seen to presuppose a metaphysically hospitable universe where normally people need not suffer innocent misery and deprivation--so that such a condition is usually the result of (a) negligence or (b) the violation of Lockean rights (that has made self-development and commerce impossible)--the occasional departures from this typical circumstance of people will have to be seen as an emergency.

Normally, then, persons cannot be said to "lack the opportunities and resources to satisfy their own basic needs." Even if we grant that some poor persons could offer nothing to anyone that would merit adequate returns enabling them to carry on with their lives and perhaps even flourish, there is still the other possibility open to most actual, known hard cases, namely, seeking help.

This is a recourse that libertarians consider morally proper. Most advocates of welfare rights forget about this. I am not speaking of the cases we know, namely, people who drop out of school, get an unskilled job, marry and have kids, only to find that their personal choice of inadequate preparation for life leaves them destitute. "Ought" implies "can" must not be treated ahistorically--some people's lack of current options is a function of their failure to have exercised previous options prudently and wisely.

We are speaking here of the "truly needy," to use a shop-worn but still useful phrase--those who have never been able to help themselves and are not now helpless from their own neglect. Are such people being treated unjustly, rather than uncharitably, ungenerously, indecently, or in some other respect immorally, when the rich who know about their plight prevent their efforts to take from them what they truly need if they refuse to seek help peacefully?

Contrary to what Sterba suggests, there is much that persons can and should do in those plausible, non-emergency situations that can be considered typical, apart from attempting to encroach upon, abridge, or violate the private property rights of the rich. The destitute should appeal for support, for help, for assistance, from all those rich who seem to have an inordinate amount of wealth that they do not need.

Consider that when one's car breaks down on a remote roadway, it would be unreasonable to expect one not to seek a phone or some way of escaping one's problem. Clearly, one ought to at least obtain the use of a phone. Should one break into the home of a perfect stranger living nearby? Or ought one to ask for the use of the phone of such a person as a favor? "Ought" implies "can" is surely satisfied here--actual practice makes this quite evident. When someone is suffering from misfortune and there are plenty of others who are not, and the poor person has no other avenue for obtaining help than to obtain it from others, it would not be unreasonable to ask the poor to seek such help as might surely be forthcoming. We cannot assume here that the rich are all callous--supporting and gaining advantage from the institution of private property by no means implies that one lacks the virtue of generosity. The rich are no more immune to virtue than the poor to vice--at least there is no reason to assume any such discriminatory outlook.

The poor typically have other options than to violate the rights of the rich. "Ought" implies "can" is satisfiable by the moral imperative that the poor ought to seek help, not loot. There is then no injustice in the rich preventing the poor from seeking such loot, by trying to violate the right to private property. "Ought" implies "can" is fully satisfied if the poor can take the kind of actions that would gain them the satisfaction of their basic needs, and this action could well be asking for help.

And all along here I have been talking about the helplessly poor, ones who through no neglect of their own, nor again through any rights violation of others who ought to be prosecuted and made to compensate for their criminal acts, are destitute. I am, in short, taking the hard cases seriously, where violation of "ought" implies "can" would appear to be most likely.

What I am not accepting, however, is that such cases are typical. I would consider them extremely rare. And even rarer are those cases in which all avenues regarded legitimate from the libertarian point of view have been exhausted, including appealing for help.

We must remember that the bulk of poverty in the world is not the result of natural disaster or disease. Rather it is political oppression, whereby people throughout many of the world's countries are legally not permitted to look out for themselves in production and trade. The famines in Africa and India, the poverty in the same countries and in Central and Latin America, as well as in China, the Soviet Union, Poland, Rumania, and so forth, are not the result of lack of charity but of oppression, the kind that those who have the protection of the U.S. Constitution, that does not guarantee welfare rights, are not experiencing. Critics of the document fail to realize that the first requirement of men and women to ameliorate their hardship is to be free of other people's oppression, not to be free to take from other people what they own.

The Just Self-Protection of the Rich

So there is no injustice in the rich preventing the poor from encroaching upon their right to private property, nor any justice in the poor conducting themselves in a way that implies such encroachment. "Ought" implies "can" is fully satisfied if the poor can typically take the kind of actions that could gain the satisfaction of their basic needs, and this action could well be asking for help.

Of course, there would be immorality if the rich would fail to help out when this is clearly no sacrifice for them. However, even their refusal cannot be judged categorically immoral. Charity or generosity is not a categorical imperative, even for the rich. There are more basic moral principles that might require the rich to refuse to be charitable--e.g., if they are embarked on the protection of their freedom or just society by the use of most of the wealth. Courage can be more important than charity or benevolence or compassion. But a discussion of the ranking of moral virtues could take us far along. Suffice it to note that one reason many critics of libertarianism find their own cases persuasive is that they think the libertarian can only subscribe to political principles or values. But this is wrong.[16]

I wish to reiterate here that there can be emergency cases in which no alternative to disregarding the rights of others is available. But these are extremely rare, not at all the sort invoked by critics such as Sterba. I have in mind that typical desert island case where instantaneous action, with only one violent alternative faces persons--the sort we know from the law books in which the issue is one of virtually immediate life and death. These are not cases, to repeat the phrase quoted from Locke by H.L.A. Hart, "where peace is possible." They are discussed in the libertarian literature and considerable progress has been made in integrating them with the concerns of law and politics. Suffice it to note here that since we are discussing law and politics, which are general, systematic approaches to how we normally ought to live with each other in human communities, these emergency situations do not aid us except as limiting cases. "Hard cases make bad law!" And not surprisingly many famous court cases illustrate just this point as they confront these kinds of cases now and then after they have come to light within the framework of civilized society but do so in an exceptional fashion--e.g., by finding defendants guilty of murder but immediately pardoning them!

Assault on Human Dignity

Let me briefly turn to the case from Nancy Davis and explain why it does not suffice to defend any kind of paternalist statist interference, assuming the case was introduced to help do that.

It seems to me that we owe it to the "lonely, shy and insecure individual" not to interfere beyond the bounds that respect her autonomy and independence, lest we relegate her to the status of a child, which by the example given she clearly is not. There are of course some people who are psychologically vulnerable to con artistry. There are many marriages and other relationships most of us have encountered in which the kind of situation Davis and Sterba have in mind with their example is evident.

Yet I do not understand why such situations make it morally permissible to take the responsibility for sound behavior out of the hands of the vulnerable person. If there is any meaning to the idea of human dignity it surely must be that any adult who is not crucially incapacitated--*incapable* of rational judgment in terms of the disciplines concerned with determining criteria for this--ought not to have her power of choice taken from her.

Doing so is a kind of kidnapping, assault, dehumanization, or the like.[17] It seems to me to evidence considerably less confidence in human nature, i.e., individual human beings, to seriously entertain the idea that some of them need to have their judgments made subservient to others. Moreover, it is a self-defeating idea to boot, since if some could require this, surely others might also, and those who do the interfering are not immune. (Here we should note the economist's insight that failures of the market are rarely if ever remedied by political means, since failures of politics tend to be far more costly and irreversible.[18])

Incidentally, despite my efforts to rebut Sterba's cases in support of the welfare statist implications of Lockean libertarianism, I do not for a moment doubt that there are some difficulties with this view. Indeed, I would maintain that any view regarding the best understanding we can obtain in any area of inquiry will probably have some difficulties--borderline cases that will not quite fit the general principles being offered. This is true in the hard, soft and human sciences.

My suggestion here is that we pay less heed to that fact than to how the various theories compare in comprehensiveness, consistency, practicability, and other qualities that apply to the field in question. On that score I would maintain that Lockean libertarianism is a principled system fraught with far fewer problems that should nag us than welfare state liberalism, socialism, communism, fascism and other social viewpoints in contention in our time.

It seems to me that I have now made the points needed to call into question Sterba's efforts to discredit the libertarian tendency of the U.S. Constitution. Indeed, had I been asked to discuss the merits and demerits of that radical document, I would have done virtually the opposite of what Sterba chose to do--I would have praised the libertarian tendencies and condemned those that compromise them, including the recent trend of the Supreme Court to fail to find in the U.S. Constitution grounds for resisting the doctrine of state rights that legally sanctions abridgement of the implicit right to privacy of every individual. I have by no means clinched the case for the negative, so to speak, but I have tried to suggest some reasons why the affirmative position placed before us by Sterba should be rejected.

Let me end my remarks with a quote from the late Sam Ervin, Jr., who understood the U.S. Constitution somewhat as I do:

> The Founding Fathers desired above all things to secure to the people in a written Constitution every right which they had wrested from autocratic rulers while they were struggling for their right to self-rule and freedom from tyranny. Their knowledge of history gave them the wisdom to know that this objective could be accomplished only in a government of laws, i.e., a government which rules by certain, constant, and uniform laws rather than by the arbitrary, uncertain, and inconstant wills of impatient men who happen to occupy for a fleeting moment of time legislative, executive, or judicial offices.[19]

NOTES

1. Quoted in Harry V. Jaffa, *How to Think About the American Revolution*. (Durham NC: Carolina Academic Press, 1978), p. 41 (from *The Collected Works of Abraham Lincoln* [R. Basler ed., 1953], pp. 108-15).

2. See, in particular, James Sterba, "A Libertarian Justification for the Welfare State," *Social Theory and Practice* II (Fall, 1985), pp. 285-306. I will be referring to this essay as well as to a more developed version of the essay within this volume.

3. H.L.A. Hart, "Are There Any Natural Rights?" *Philosophical Review*, 64 (1955), p. 175.

4. See, for my own discussion, Tibor R. Machan, *Human Rights and Human Liberties*. (Chicago: Nelson-Hall, 1975), pp. 213-222; "Prima Facie versus Natural (Human) Rights," *Journal of Value Inquiry*, 10 (1976), pp. 119-31; "Human Rights: Some Points of Clarification," *Journal of Critical Analysis*, 5 (1973), pp. 30-39.

5. Sterba, op. cit., "A Libertarian Justification," p. 295.

6. *Ibid*.

7. Ayn Rand, "Value and Rights," in J. Hospers, ed., *Readings in Introductory Philosophical Analysis*. (Englewood Cliffs NJ: Prentice-Hall, 1968), p. 382.

8. John Rawls, *A Theory of Justice*. (Cambridge MA: Harvard University Press, 1971), pp. 101-2. For a discussion of the complexities in the differential attainments of members of various ethnic groups--often invoked as evidence for the injustice of a capitalist system, see Thomas Sowell, Ethnic America: A History (New York: Basic Books, 1981). There appears to be a persistent prejudicial view in welfare state proponents' writings when it comes to crediting people with the ability of extricating themselves from poverty without any special political assistance. The whole idea behind the right to negative liberty is to set people free from others so as to pursue their progressive goals, not to guarantee for them success which is, in any case, a hopeless, utopian dream, not sound public policy, as the failure of welfare statist and socialist systems illustrates. This is the ultimate teleological justification of Lockean libertarian natural rights. See Tibor R. Machan, Human Rights and Human Liberties: A Radical Reconsideration of the American Political Tradition. (Chicago: Nelson-Hall, 1975). Consider also this thought from Herbert Spencer:

> The feeling which vents itself in "poor fellow!" on seeing one in agony, excludes the thought of "bad fellow," which might at another time arise. Naturally, then, if the wretched are unknown or but vaguely known, all the demerits they may have are ignored: and thus it happens that when the miseries of the

> poor are dilated upon, they are thought of as the miseries of the deserving poor, instead of being thought of as the miseries of undeserving poor, which in large measure they should be. Those whose hardships are set forth in pamphlets and proclaimed in sermons and speeches which echo throughout society, are assumed to be all worthy souls, grievously wronged; and none of them are thought of as bearing the penalties of their own misdeeds. (*Man versus the State* [Caldwell ID: Caxton Printers, 1940], p. 22).

Consider also the following case: a vicious criminal is being chased by the police and falls and breaks a limb, whereupon witnesses are horrified and feel terrible at the sight of this. What this illustrates is that we normally give people the benefit of doubt about their misfortunes. But upon being informed of their neglience or ill will, our attitudes and thus our emotions can easily change.

9. Tibor R. Machan, "Ethics vs. Coercion: Morality or Just Values?" in L.H. Rockwell, Jr., et. al., ed., *Man, Economy and Liberty: Essays in Honor of Murray N. Rothbard*. (Munchen, Germany: Philosophia Verlag, 1988), forthcoming.

10. John Kekes, " 'Ought Implies Can' and Two Kinds of Morality," *The Philosophical Quarterly* 34 (1984), pp. 479-97.

11. Tibor R. Machan, "Ethics vs. Coercion." In a vegetable garden or even in a forest, there can be good and bad, but no morally good things and morally evil things (outside the people who might be there).

12. Sterba, op. cit., "A Libertarian Justification," pp. 295-96.

13. For a more elaborate rendition of this kind of defense of paternalism and welfare statism, see Steven Kelman, "Regulation and Paternalism," in T.R. Machan and M.B. Johnson, eds., *Rights and Regulations, Ethical, Political, and Economic Issues*. Cambridge MA: Ballinger Publ. Co., 1983), pp. 217-48.

14. Robert Nozick, *Anarchy, State, and Utopia*. (New York: Basic Books, 1974), p. 57. See, also, Tibor R. Machan, "Conditions for Rights, Sphere of Authority," *Journal of Human Relations* 19 (1971), pp. 184-87. I argue in this paper that "within the context of a legal system where the *sphere of authority* of individuals and groups of individuals cannot be delineated independently of the sphere of authority of the public as a whole, there is an inescapable conflict of rights specified by the same legal system" (186). See, also, Tibor R. Machan, "The Virtue of Freedom in Capitalism," *The Journal of Applied Philosophy* 3 (1986), pp. 49-58, and Douglas J. Den Uyl, "Freedom and Virtue," in T.R. Machan, ed., *The Main Debate: Communism versus Capitalism*. (New York: Random House, 1987), pp. 200-216. This last essay is especially pertinent to the understanding of the ethical or moral merits of coercion and coerced conduct. To wit, "coercive charity" amounts to an oxymoron.

15. See, Machan, op. cit., "The Virtue of Freedom in Capitalism" and "Private Property and the Decent Society," in J.K. Roth and R.C. Whittemore, eds., *Ideology and American Experience* (Washington DC: The Washington Institute Press, 1986).

16. E.g., James Fishkin, *Tyranny and Legitimacy*. (Baltimore MD: John Hopkins University Press, 1979). Cf. Tibor R. Machan, "Fishkin on Nozick's Absolute Rights," *Journal of Libertarian Studies* 6 (1982), pp. 317-20.

17. Tibor R. Machan, "Human Dignity and the Law," *DePaul Law Review*, 26 (1977), pp. 807-832. I discuss the concept of unconscionability in this paper, which has usually meant "an absence of meaningful choice on the part of the parties together with contract terms which are unreasonably favorable to the other party" *(Williams v. Walker-Thomas Furniture Co.*, 350 F 2nd 445 [D.C. Cir. 1965].

18. James Buchanan and Gordon Tullock, *The Calculus of Consent*. (Ann Arbor MI: University of Michigan Press, 1962).

19. Sam Ervin, Jr., "Judicial Verbicide: An Affront to the Constitution," *Modern Age*, 25 (1981), p. 235.

A BRIEF REPLY TO THREE COMMENTATORS

James P. Sterba

I would like to thank my three commentators for their valuable and insightful comments and make just a few responses to help clarify the issues.

First of all, in my argument against the libertarian, my aim was not to initially establish a positive right to welfare, that is, a right to receive welfare from the rich. Rather I initially tried to establish what I would call a negative right to welfare, that, a right not to be interfered with when taking from the surplus possessions of the rich what is required to meet one's basic needs. However, if I can establish the legitimacy of a negative right to welfare against the libertarian, then I think libertarians will have good reasons to set up institutions guaranteeing positive rights to welfare as well. This is because once libertarians come to be subject to the discretion of rightholders in choosing when and how to exercise these rights, libertarians will tend to favor the only morally legitimate way of preventing the exercise of such rights: they will institute adequate positive rights to welfare which will then take precedence over the exercise of negative rights to welfare.

Second, with respect to my argument for the poor's negative right not to be interfered with when taking from the surplus possessions of the rich what they require to meet their basic needs, I claimed that such a right would have force when the application of the "ought" implies "can" principle shows it to be preferable to the right of the rich not to be interfered with when using their surplus for luxury purposes. In commenting on this argument, Tibor Machan accepts the moral relevance of the "ought" implies "can" principle as I formulate it. And, in his unrevised comments, he just claims that the principle does not support the action of the poor in my example because the poor do not lack the opportunity and resources to satisfy their basic needs since they could "appeal for support, for help, for assistance, from all those rich who seem to have an inordinate amount of wealth that they do not need." However, in his revised comments, Machan recognizes that in my example, as I envisioned it, this option has also been exhausted. Accordingly, in his revised comments, Machan now admits that the rights proclaimed by libertarians do not apply in the conflict situation I envisioned. His current defense is that such situations are *untypical*.

My response is twofold. First, given that proclaimed libertarian rights no longer apply in such situations, there is still the question of what should be done when one is in such a situation. My contention is that in such situations the liberty of the poor has moral priority over the liberty of the rich despite the fact that the rich usually have the power to enforce a resolution favoring themselves. Moreover, to let power decide in such situations, as some libertarians seem inclined to do, is simply to abandon a moral point of view. Here, if anywhere, morality should decide.

Second, such situations are not untypical. To assume that they are is to assume that it is *always* in the interest of the rich to provide or permit sufficient opportunities for the poor so that they can meet their basic needs. But surely this assumption is too good to be true. Surely, the interests of the rich and the poor conflict, and, where there are great disparities between the rich and the poor, that conflict will be widespread. Thus, in the United States, the conflict between the rich and the poor that I am envisioning will be typical at least until the basic needs of the poor are adequately provided for by constitutional rights to welfare and equal opportunity.

Turning to Carlin Romano's comments, Romano thinks it is quite easy to derive rights to equal opportunity and welfare from various political ideals by simply tailoring one's premises to get the conclusions one wants. Having been involved with the project of exploring the implications of alternative political ideals for some time now, I think Romano underestimates the difficulty here, but, in any case, with respect to the libertarian ideal, I think it is clear that I have not unfairly construed the premises of the view because Machan, whose libertarian credentials are impeccable, basically agrees with me on the premises of the libertarian view. Our disagreement concerns what conclusions are to be drawn from those premises, not the premises themselves.

Second, Romano addresses my claim that the U.S. Constitution does not actually guarantee rights to welfare and equal opportunity, and, in fact, he argues both for and against the claim. He argues against the claim by contending that given the evolutionary nature of the Constitution, it is possible that a Supreme Court somewhere down the line may find rights to welfare and equal opportunity embedded in the Constitution. He argues for the claim by contending that virtually throughout our entire constitutional history, even during the New Deal period, the idea that the U.S. Constitution guaranteed rights to welfare and equal opportunity was never seriously entertained. Now I think his argument for my claim overcomes his argument against it.

Third, Romano thinks that with respect to the Constitution we should think about rights to equal opportunity and welfare as "provided rights" rather than "guaranteed rights." But he uses the term "provided rights" ambiguously. By it he means rights that the government could provide--not necessarily does provide--and this links up with his view that a constitution should tell a government what it can do, not what it must do. The problem I have with this stance is that I do not see any reason why the U.S. Constitution should be open-ended just where our political ideals are not. If our political ideals say that rights to welfare and equal opportunity are basic requirements of justice, as I have argued they do, then I see no reason why our Constitution should not similarly contain these same requirements of justice. A Constitution that simply permits the basic requirements of justice is a constitution that also permits and tolerates basic injustices, as our Constitution in fact does, and, for that reason, I think it deserves the label "a fundamentally flawed document."

Of course, incorporating rights to equal opportunity and welfare rights into the Constitution involves the enforcement of morality, but it is the enforcement of public morality, that is the basic requirements of justice, not private morality that is in issue here. Even so, it should be stressed that my immediate goal is not to get a constitutional amendment introduced into Congress. Rather my immediate goal is to convince people that the political ideals they actually endorse support rights to welfare and equal opportunity. In my judgment, the repair of the Constitution will only be possible and practical after people come to appreciate the actual requirements of the ideals they endorse.

Happily my response to Robert Moffat's comments, which accompanied an earlier presentation of my paper, can be briefest of all. In the present version of the paper, I stress that the implementation of constitutional rights to welfare and equal opportunity should occur primarily through the legislature and only secondarily through the courts. That is why the focus of my paper was on establishing that rights to welfare and equal opportunity are the fundamental requirements of the moral and political ideals we endorse. For only when the realization that such rights do follow from the ideals we endorse is widespread in our society can the possibility of implementing such rights at the constitutional level be realistically faced because only then would the popular support required for legislative action be present.

Obviously, there is more that I can and should say in response to my commentators, but, for brevity's sake, I will simply thank them again for helping me clarify these points and stop there.

LIST OF CONTRIBUTORS

Aryeh Botwinick
Department of Political Science
Temple University
Philadelphia, PA

John Peterman
Department of Philosophy
William Paterson College
Wayne, NJ

John Ryder
Department of Philosophy
State University of New York
College at Cortland
Cortland, NY

Sterling Harwood
Department of Philosophy
Cornell University
Ithaca, NY

David Fortunoff
Department of Philosophy
State University of New York
Stoney Brook, NY

John Waide
Department of Humanities
Christian Brothers College
Memphis, TN

Edward S. Petry, Jr.
Department of Philosophy
Bentley College
Waltham, MA

Michael Eldridge
Discipline of Philosophy
Spring Hill College
Mobile, AL

E. Paul Colella
Department of Philosophy
Xavier University
Cincinnati, OH

William W. Clohesy
Department of Philosophy and Religion
University of Northern Iowa
Cedar Falls, IA

Mary L. Sabato
Department of Philosophy
Villanova University
Villanova, PA

Morris Grossman
Department of Philosophy
Fairfield University
Fairfield, CT

Robert Ginsberg
Department of Philosophy
Pennsylvania State University
Media, PA

Frederic R. Kellogg
General Counsel
National Endowment for the Arts
Washington, DC

Christopher B. Gray
Department of Philosophy
Concordia University
Montreal, Quebec, Canada

James P. Sterba
Department of Philosophy
University of Notre Dame
Notre Dame, IN

Carlin Romano
Book Editor, Critic
Philadelphia Inquirer
Philadelphia, PA

Robert C. L. Moffat
College of Law
University of Florida
Gainesville, FL

Tibor R. Machan
Department of Philosophy
Auburn University
Auburn, AL

INDEX OF LEGISLATIVE AND JUDICIAL CITATIONS: AUTHORITATIVE TEXTS

INDEX OF NAMES

INDEX OF SUBJECTS

STUDIES IN SOCIAL AND POLITICAL THEORY

1. J.W. Cooke, **The American Tradition of Liberty 1800-1860: From Jefferson to Lincoln**
2. Yeager Hudson and Creighton Peden (eds.), **Philosophical Essays on the Ideas of a Good Society (Social Philosophy Today; Number 1)**
3. James Sterba and Creighton Peden (eds.), **Freedom, Equality, and Social Change: Philosophical Essays (Social Philosophy Today; Number 2)**
4. Christopher Gray, **Philosophical Reflections on the United States Constitution: A Collection of Bicentennial Essays**
5. Robert Kocis, **A Critical Appraisal of Sir Isaiah Berlin's Political Philosophy: Liberty in a World of Uncertainty**
6. Barry Cooper, **The Restoration of Political Science and the Crisis of Modernity**